PRA

MAGDALE

M000078830

"*Magdalena Moments* is the anticipated sequel to *The Birth of Magdalena*, both very intimate accounts of trauma and recovery, of birth and postpartum, and of raising children and the opportunity for deep personal discovery that parenting provides. *Magdalena Moments* takes the reader on yet another transformative journey of self-discovery by the author, through personal experiences examined through the lens of courage, faith and love. The author writes with honesty and wisdom, revealing her wide-open heart and her deep authenticity, which encourages the reader to explore their own. The structure of the book takes us on a journey through the body's 7 Chakras, as they correlate to the author's 7 Mothering Missions, and each of the 7 chapters contain interactive exercises which help forge a path to our own discoveries. Mb Antevasin's powerful journey is one that encourages the reader to embark upon their very own. *Magdalena Moments* is the lantern we can use to light our way."

~*Tisha Graham CPM, CCE, CD, CLC*

"I found The Birth of Magdalena through my work as a birth and postpartum doula, and I loved being able to pick up the story with Magdalena Moments. I feel like I traveled with Michelle through her childhood and becoming a mother and it's great to see how she managed life and healing as a mom. She has learned so much and I am glad that she wants to share it with us. The "Things to Try" at the end of each chapter helped me to take steps on my own healing journey."

~*Sarah McCormick, Sweet Fern Doula*

"As a mother of three, Magdalena Moments spoke to my heart. Mothers who are doing the messy, rewarding work of tending young children need reminders that motherhood is a journey, that we grow both as mothers and as our own selves as our children grow. This book is a must-read for any mother in the trenches looking for guidance in mapping out their mothering journey."

~Nancy Cavillones

Magdalena

moments

Magdalena *moments*

7 Steps into Becoming Your True Self

Book Two in Magdalena's Journey

MB ANTEVASIN

KAT BIGGIE
PRESS

Cover Design: Michelle Fairbanks, Fresh Design
Interior Design:Write.Publish.Sell
Photography Credit: Catherine Veltum

All artwork handdrawn in black pen by MB Antevasin

Published by Kat Biggie Press
ISBN: 9781948604062

Library of Congress Control Number: 2018941185

10 9 8 7 6 5 4 3 2 1

Dedication

This book is dedicated to the daughters, the sisters, the mothers and the grandmothers that form intricate circles of support around us all.

Contents

Acknowledgements

This book would not have been possible without seven powerful circles of support for this journey.

~ I would like to thank my parents and grandparents who gave me so many tools for my journey. My mom inspired me to love both science and spirituality and let me know that I didn't have to choose one or the other. My Dad taught me the art of storytelling and how to just keep climbing another mountain. My grandparents taught me how to be strong and how to feed the people that you love.

~ I also want to thank my brothers and sister who will always be close to my heart, even when we are miles apart, and my brothers and sisters in law who have come to be a part of our story.

~ I owe so much to all of the people that I've met along the way that have inspired and encouraged me, even though many of them will never know how much those moments mattered.

~ I want to honor the powerful women that have gone before me to light the way, and the ones who have left breadcrumbs along the path, and the ones who have stumbled along beside me through the good times and the bad.

~ I want to thank Kat Biggie Press for helping me to empower and inspire others through sharing my story. I am honored to be in the company of so many amazing women, many who have become experts in things that they never wanted to learn, but they survived and they chose to use their knowledge and their gifts to reach back and help others up some of those hardest parts of the path.

~Most of all I need to thank my husband who has taken this journey with me. We have weathered the storms together and I know that I would never be able to do this kind of deep work without him by my side.

~Finally, none of this healing, mothering journey would be possible without my four children. I used to wonder when they would come and what they would be like and now I can't picture a life without them in it. I was so blessed to be able to grow them in my belly and birth them into this world, and now I am holding space as they grow into their full selves. I am enjoying the mess and the noise of our crazy, beautiful life together as I know that all too soon the house will be much emptier and quieter.

In those moments when I need to find my courage, I look towards that future where I can fully be my true self, and I am learning to trust that it will all work towards my good in the end even though the path takes some interesting twists and turns along the way. I know that I would never be able to make up a story like this, so I simply appreciate each detail as I spiral through these patterns and take notice of life's synchronicities. I am looking forward to seeing where the journey takes me next.

Preface

Here I am, sitting at another kitchen table, talking about births and deaths and sharing the stories of life and marveling about just how profound and important it all is. The girl that I once was is a fading memory. A dozen years have passed. Grandma has passed too. And while I was still processing my birth story, my babies grew taller than me somehow. They say that the days can seem to be endless, but the years pass quickly. That is never truer than when you reflect on your mothering journey.

The past few years have certainly not been easy. My family was brought to a deeper understanding of death, but through that we have come to a fuller understanding of the true meaning of life. Death is like birth in that it is much messier and even more meaningful than you ever imagined. It is heavier than you can fathom, but then you go and make the sandwiches.

I always wanted to be a mom and run a household.

I love taking care of children. I had helped to raise my siblings and I had been a babysitter and worked at a daycare. I have even worked at a preschool and taught the little ones at church on Sunday. But I also wanted to grow a baby in my belly and to know that baby better than anyone else ever could. I wanted to hold them in my arms, and love them forever. I am eternally grateful that I was able to fulfill that dream. It is always interesting for me to look back at how my reality often plays out quite differently than my dream of how it would be.

I am glad that I wrote that book when I did, because I cannot even speak in her voice anymore. I have moved down the path and around the bend. Some days, I remember her and I look back to see how far I have come. I can't see very far into the darkness of that wood, so I turn around and look back into the light ahead. But I am the *Antevasin*. I am the spiritual seeker living at the edge of two worlds. And I can carry the candle and light the way for others to follow.

I shared my birth stories in The Birth of Magdalena in an attempt to further the discussion about just how profound every birth is, and just how complex our stories can be when viewed across time. I wanted to address every comment that I heard that just didn't make sense with my story. I wanted to answer those complicated questions that were left hanging in the air. I wrote it for the women who didn't seem to understand my meaning, but even more so for the ones that did. I hoped they would not feel so alone. For anyone who saw my older, wiser self standing in her power and speaking her truth and thought, "I could never be that brave." I wanted to tell her the story of how far I had come. I wanted to leave my breadcrumbs on the path to inspire her, to give her strength and to support her as she takes steps on her own personal journey towards healing.

So that is where I left you last. I was stumbling along on my spiritual journey, looking for which path to take next. I realized that the Magdalena from my dreams was not meant to be my daughter after all, but was in fact an image of my future self. When I first had that realization it was awesome in the truest sense of the word. I was in awe -- dumbfounded, actually. I kind of just sat with that for a while but then knew that I would have to find a way, and find the courage to become her, somehow.

I could see her when I turned inwards in prayer, but it was as if she was not only walking along ahead of me, but also across this wide river. I had no idea how to get across that river so I just kept taking baby steps forward and hoped that maybe someday there would be a really obvious bridge that led from where I was to where I was going. I looked for clues about which way to go. I was determined to say "yes" to each opportunity that presented itself. Some of those opportunities were so far outside of my comfort zone, but I knew that if I could just take a leap that it would be good for my learning and my growth. After my amazingly empowering homebirth I knew that I could trust the power of my faith. I knew that if I could visualize it, I could make it happen. But I also knew that the story would unfold in its own way and I watched with curiosity as each new chapter of my life was written.

In the meantime, I was busy being the mother to four beautiful, young children. I was discovering that it was a much bigger job than I had anticipated. I think that I had understood that it was huge, but like many enormous things, you could only really look at one aspect of it at a time. I find that many people argue about which description is the best, but they are all just looking at motherhood from different angles. Reading the moms fighting with each other in the comments on social media or trying to put labels on themselves or others often reminds me of "The Blind

Men and the Elephant." In that fable, each Blind man describes different parts of an elephant (large ears, big feet, little tail, etc.), arguing over whose description is correct, when in fact they are each experiencing only one aspect of the whole thing. (1) Our perceptions may all be correct, and we can only speak from our own perspective, but we can learn to put the pieces together and see a little more of the big picture. So while there is no right answer when it comes to mothering, I sat down one day and wrote a list for myself of all of my biggest goals (which are consequently all of the biggest challenges) of being a mother.

The idea had actually come to me in a dream, and when I completed mapping out my mothering vision, I realized that there were seven major themes. This corresponded with what I had been reading about the seven levels of spiritual healing and about how we have seven energy centers in our bodies. So, I knew it was significant when I jotted down seven themes. If you have never heard of the seven energy centers in the body, also known as chakras, you are not alone. I will always remember the moment that I first heard about how in addition to our physical systems, we also have an energetic system. When we feel drained from giving too much of "ourselves," too much of our own energy, or spending too much energy on the wrong things, it is the response of this energetic system. This understanding helped me to make sense of what I had been feeling. It was good to finally find a way to put it into words. It was even better to realize that by learning to understand the patterns, I would be able to start feeling better.

Reading about the types of health conditions that develop when people have blocks in certain energy centers explained so many things. I finally had an answer to why I had developed my physical symptoms at painful times in my life. I hadn't known how to process what was happening. During those traumatic moments, I didn't know how to release my feelings, so they got stuck, blocking the flow of health, and causing disease. The stories that I had been carrying for each of those pivotal moments, were not only carried in my narrative memory, they were carried in my cellular memory as well. It made sense that I could feel them so deeply, because the wounds were so deep.

I shared about how I had that revelation, and how I started searching for meaning and taking steps towards healing, in my first book. I was amazed to find such clear answers on chakra charts, when the medical specialists and surgeons hadn't been able to give me any answers for all those years. I can look back and remember the correlations between emotional pain and physical manifestations. I recall that right after I got in trouble for speaking up, I actually developed physical blockages in my mouth that prevented me from talking. It is amazing how our bodies use this information from our emotional pain to learn how to keep us physically safe. Learning to see the patterns in that way, opened my eyes to a new way of seeing the world. This new realization that I could really fully heal, not just learn to manage my symptoms, gave me hope that I could break free from those old patterns. I felt empowered to break the cycle, for myself and for my children.

I wanted to take care of my children's physical, financial, social, emotional, mental, and spiritual health as well as helping them each to align with their soul purpose and learn to follow their passion. They each have their own unique gifts and their own set of challenges and I try to nurture and guide them. I try to create opportunities for each of them while also teaching them to listen to the wisdom of their own intuition. Of course the challenge is to do this differently and simultaneously for each completely different child, all while they are quick to point out every nuance of how it is "not fair."

These were my core beliefs about where I should spend my time and energy as their mother. Even as I named them, I knew that there were so many factors outside of my control. I had to accept that it does not mean that I am a bad mom if I don't accomplish all of them perfectly. The path never seems to go the way that I am expecting, but I still like to have a goal to strive for anyway. When I am hiking a mountain, even if I don't have a map, I just keep putting one foot in front of the other and as long as I keep going upwards, I trust that I am moving in the right direction. Sometimes the trail needs to double back or take me sideways for a while though, because it is easier in the long run than trying to climb up a huge cliff. In the real world, the path is seldom straight and uneventful, but that is also what makes it interesting. When it comes to mothering, in addition to all of the complexities in the world that are outside of my control, each child is on their own journey, and they have their own stories to tell. In the quiet moments, I try to remember to stop and enjoy the view and look back at just how far I have come.

After I wrote down my ideas about this complex task of being their mother, I noticed that I had written down 7 things. I wondered if the list had any similarity to the themes that had come up for me as I learned about the attributes of each energy center. I looked more closely at each chakra. I learned to understand my past, clear those old blockages, and let healthy energy flow again. I looked at what I had written about what I wanted to do for my children, and rearranged them to line up with the seven energy centers, and found that I had unknowingly covered all of those themes.

My Mothering Mission

To Raise Children that are:

1. **Physically**: *Healthy and Alive*

2. **Financially:** *Secure and Responsible*

3. **Socially**: *Aware and Respectful*

4. **Passionately**: *Loving and Purposeful*

5. **Emotionally**: *Safe and Heard*

6. **Mentally**: *Stimulated and Challenged*

7. **Spiritually**: *Connected and Seeking*

When we are born, we begin to move through seven year cycles of development, laying down patterns for our physical, emotional and spiritual health as we spiral through the seasons between each birthday. The themes that we focus on each year coincide with the energy centers. We start by putting down roots in that first year as we learn to depend on our family to keep us safe and warm. We feel how strong those roots are in our first energy center. Conversely, if we do not feel like we are on firm footing, we feel that in the aches and pains that develop in our legs. As I pay more attention, I notice more and more ways in which our language has phrases for these ways in which we hold this subconscious information in our bodies. As we move through these levels, we create more memories, year after year. (*See Appendix*)

Seeing what I want for my children at each phase partly comes from feeling what is lacking in my own life. Each child has a fundamental need to feel loved, to feel safe, and to feel important. With each passing age as my own children grew, I remembered moments from my own childhood where I did not feel heard, or seen, or significant. Looking back at those stories through adult eyes, I could understand how that happened, and I could forgive. I gave myself permission to grieve, and to accept that my needs were totally normal and natural. After I allowed myself to really feel and acknowledge the truth of each of those stories, I was able to let energy flow to those parts of myself that had been stuck in that moment and then I could feel my physical health start to improve. It's kind of like when you absentmindedly twist a rubber band around your finger and then notice that your fingertip is red and throbbing. When you acknowledge the problem and remove the block, you can let healthy flow return, but it may still be uncomfortable for a while to make sure that you remember not to do that again.

I try to raise my kids from a position at the crossroads. We are involved in the mainstream society just enough so that we can understand and navigate the current cultural landscape. My children attend public school and we go to church as a family, but I also want them to stay connected to their own guidance and their own wisdom. I hope that they will stay oriented and find their own way. We are at that edge between worlds, so they can always see that there is more than meets the eye. They can question and challenge the status quo. And all of that hands-on, attached, responsive parenting that we did when they were small really starts to pay off when they are forging their way into the world, a little more each day and each year. (I'm going to write this book quickly because before I know it, they will be driving and applying to colleges!)

We spent so much time and energy when they were newborns and toddlers teaching them that they can trust us and that we would do everything in our power to keep them safe. We let them know in a million small ways that they can call on us, knowing that someday they may need to call on us for something huge. Because we love them, we let them follow their own path, which often leaves us on that edge of amazing pride and terrifying fear in the same moment.

In these moments, it can be hard to know what to feel, especially when you have more than one kid and feel your heart pulled in so many directions at once. Sometimes you have to do these amazingly complicated calculations really quickly in your head to choose which the biggest danger is, or find a way to split yourself in two so that you can run in two different directions. Often you have to choose between your desire and theirs. And if you are co-parenting, then you need to negotiate and make compromises with your partner and maintain that relationship at the same time. There are so many days when I feel like I am just completely failing. I always wanted to be a mom. I chose this. Now I'm messing it all up. I just can't figure out how to do it right.

But then I remind myself that I am here, I am trying, I am doing my best. I am committed to them and they know that I care and that I am always doing the best that I can in each moment. But in some of those moments I am exhausted and clueless and I just get it wrong. But I have great kids, and often when I'm having a really hard day, they'll give me a hug and tell me that it's okay. They see me and they heal my heart and my soul in so many ways.

So when I looked more deeply at those seven aspects of my mothering mission, I understood that there were places that I needed to do more of my own healing. I needed to feel more safe, secure and significant. One of the wonderful things about motherhood is that it gives you a chance to revisit each of those phases again and while recognizing the needs that your own children have, you can heal those places in yourself that had the same normal and natural need for things like nurturing touch. I know that my parents loved me, and I know that they always did the best that they could, but sometimes they did not have the tools to give me what I needed. They weren't always able to protect me, so I became hyper-vigilant about protecting my children. I see the effects of family trauma travel through the generations, creating a kind of pendulum movement. The generation that experiences the trauma tries to correct the damage, and the next generation overcorrects in the other direction. It can keep going like that for generations until it calms and balances at the center. Habits and behaviors become so established that you need to take a step back to be able to see where they originated. If you are too close to the story, it is like watching television with your face pressed up against the screen and you need to back up to gain perspective and actually see the picture.

Sometimes the trauma is specific to the family, like when the family home burned down and they all needed to start over. Sometimes the whole community was affected by a more widespread trauma like war or famine. If it is a really old story, it may be that nobody even remembers what started it all. I spent years learning my own family history and gaining perspective on my own cultural traditions and seeing how they contributed to who I am. Then I married into a family from another culture and had to start learning all over again, because my children carry those stories as well. Much of this just makes us each beautifully different in our own way, but sometimes the ways that we are experiencing the world are quite painful. Sometimes those old wounds need to finally heal. I tend to start with the painful symptoms or the problem-behaviors or limiting beliefs that are rising to the surface and calling for attention, and then try to follow the clues and find where they originated. While

I understand and forgive, I am committed to breaking those intergenerational patterns, letting go of beliefs that no longer serve me and creating new tools.

As I learned more of my family stories, I found that because of early childhood medical trauma, my parents had suffered a loss of connection with their mothers. They didn't receive the nurturing that they needed at those critical moments in their development. Without a secure, early attachment to the mother or other primary caregivers, it's hard for babies to form healthy connections later on. Although my parents cared for me and wanted what was best for me, they didn't know how to connect with me as deeply as I longed for or how to give me the nurturing that I so desperately craved. My mom had the longing and the desire to be a perfect mother, and she always tried really hard. Metaphorically speaking, my mother had picked up the bucket and carried it up the hill only to find that when she got to the top of the hill, the well was dry. I give her so much credit for all that she gave me, and now I have to take that bucket from her and go climb the next hill.

While I can only share what I know, our family story is not unique. The more I researched and dug deeper into the stories of my own family, the more I found that there were many larger trends including medical and cultural practices that had interfered with the bond between mothers and babies. Those practices were the standard of care at the time, but now we can see how they robbed the children from those generations of that caring connection to their mothers, their connection to their own intuition, and to the wisdom of their ancestors. So, even though I work on my own healing, and I am motivated to avoid passing on these patterns to my own children, I know that this is healing that needs to be done universally.

So many amazing things come in sevens. We are so accustomed to spiraling through the seven days in the week, always going back to the day on which we started. Our lives move in seven year cycles as we move through the growth and development of the seven energy centers in the body. In this book, I will take you through some of the ways in which I learned to explore the seven stages of healing and personal development. Like the powerful changes that need to occur to transform a tiny caterpillar into a magnificent butterfly, I had to take many steps on my journey to becoming more true to myself.

I moved through seven major phases of growth and transformation, while at the same time mothering my young children. I needed to acknowledge my truth and learn to love and accept myself (from my roots in my culture and family, to my self-esteem and creativity, to my identity and individuality, to finding balance at the heart of it all, to fully expressing myself and holding space for my vision, and finding inspiration for the journey.) I am now in the seventh year since I wrote the first book, hence the urgency to put pen to paper and tell you the next part of the story; the story about how I learned to embrace these *Magdalena Moments*.

Chapter 1: Rooted and Grounded

Even before we are born, we begin to put down roots. As our placenta grows with the instructions passed down from our father's family and weaves its way into the womb of our mother, we are beginning to take in information from our environment. We are rooted into the customs and beliefs, the sounds and tastes and rhythms of our tribe, our family, and our culture long before we take our first breath. After our birth, we carry with us the effects of those important first moments.

Our first energy center is referred to as our root chakra because it is our base of support and how we draw energy up from the Earth. It includes our physical support system: our legs and feet, pelvis and lower back. When you are told to be more grounded, they are referring to this energy center. They want you to be more firmly rooted into your current reality and not up in the clouds or acting spacey. Even before we are born we begin to learn the tastes that will remind us of home and we learn the rhythms of our language and our culture. After birth, we learn even more about our family values, and establish what we recognize as that feeling of home and of comfort. When we feel safe and secure and all of our physical needs are met, then we can grow with a healthy flow of energy through this root, feeling like we will be provided with all of the resources that we need to grow and to thrive. When we feel unsupported, like nobody has our back, or no place feels like home, it can show up as lower back pain, or hip/knee/foot pain or restless legs. In the first year especially, when we are still so small and helpless, so much of those feelings of being loved and supported come from a healthy attachment to our mothers and other caregivers.

I believe that even before we are conceived, our soul has its own purpose and is coming here to take a particular journey. Our soul chooses a mother and comes to be a part of a particular family. Sometimes it is for the shortest while, to touch our hearts and change us in so many ways, even if we don't consciously know how much their soul has entwined with ours. Even the shortest of lifetimes can affect us deeply. Sometimes those baby souls stay a little longer and we conceive a physical body for their spirit to dwell in for this journey. I have talked to so many mothers who have felt the soul come to be with them, dreamed of their babies, and felt their presence even before conception. And then sometimes the babies stay and grow and change us even more. We are mothers to them all, no matter how long we have together. Sometimes we birth them into this world and hold them in our arms and nurture them as they grow. It is then that our mothering journey takes on the role of parenting. But sometimes when we are asked how many children we have, we don't know whether to answer for the number of children that we are raising, the number of babies we carried, or the number of souls that have come to leave their impression on our hearts. I share my story with other mothers to let them know that this mothering journey is never simple; it is intricate and complicated and messy, but that is what makes it so profound, and so beautiful.

When those souls come to make this journey with us, their soul purpose intersects with our family stories, and they take on all of the programs and patterns that they have inherited from their ancestors. As they grow in our wombs, they take in the messages that help them to adapt to the current environment. When they are born, we hold them close and bond with them deeply so that they learn to trust us and depend on us. That trust is so important later when they start to take baby steps away from us. They need to know that we are always close and that we are keeping them safe. In those early months they are growing in their understanding of the current cultural landscape and it helps them to be oriented and grounded in this moment, but at the same time they come with their own wisdom.

The babies and their families are learning so much in these early months and years, and every time you welcome another member into your family it changes the dynamics and it changes each individual as well. Just think about how much you can tell about someone just by their birth order. Even before we are born we already have multiple roles to play as child, grandchild, sibling, cousin and so on. But it is through these complex relationships that we learn the most and are able to do the most soul growth. When we take care of each other, we are all able to use our gifts and talents and work towards fulfilling our own soul purpose. But as we know, not all families are able to always give this kind of loving nurturing and attention because they are busy attending to the most basic needs. In our biology, we are physically wired for survival, and unless we feel safe and well fed we are not going to be in a good place to take care of others. Sometimes mothers and families have to make impossible choices. But we are all doing our best.

I know in my own family history there were times when the babies could not be cared for by their own mothers. Even when those babies were physically cared for by other family members and were raised in a loving home, they may have still longed for their mothers. Sometimes the mother/baby bond was broken in those early moments after birth and the baby was able to be raised physically close to their mother, but there was an emotional distance. The children were fed and clothed, but there was no energy left to love them and make them feel important. Those feelings of abandonment and insignificance can send ripples through the generations and be felt by their children and their grandchildren. Sometimes we know the stories, and sometimes those stories are so old or just hurt so much that nobody is speaking about them anymore. In this case, our bodies still feel them, and just don't know why.

◆

We often hear of *Nature vs. Nurture* like the two concepts are completely separate and in opposition to each other. In our modern world, and certainly on television it can sometimes seem like everything is a contest or a competition. But our world is not that simple. Everything is intricately woven into a beautiful tapestry. Our roots are tangled and entwined with those closest to us and we cannot describe them without considering how they were shaped by both the nature of the environment in which they grew and the nurturing that they received. We are particularly vulnerable to those influences in those early, formative years of growth and development.

The environment plays a large part in establishing your patterns for lifelong health and wellness. The quality of the care that you receive, the purity of your air and water, and the safety of your home are all factors that play a part in determining your physical health. But in all the discussion about environment, we tend to picture the world at large, when in fact we need to be looking more closely. Environmentalism can be described as something out there, as if it is separate from us, and not an integral part of our existence. When the experts speak of the effects of the environment on our health, we need to realize that the environment of the womb in which we grow affects our health more than anything that we encounter for the rest of our life.

Another debate that we hear in this discussion, especially when searching for the root cause of a chronic disease, is about *Genes vs. Environment*. But as time goes by and research methods change, scientists sometimes find that things like heart disease or diabetes that they've been calling a chronic disease might actually have been caused by a bacteria or a virus. For example, maybe you had a mild infection and so many years went by before you had additional symptoms and you never put two and two together. You wouldn't think that the fever you had as a child had any connection to the chronic illness that you have now. It isn't until a scientist picks apart the data and looks at it from a population perspective that patterns start to emerge. Sometimes it seems like it takes a long time for the science to confirm what the grandmothers have been telling us all along. It is not only about what happened to us in our infancy and childhood. The researchers are just starting to pay more attention to our earliest environment, when we were just a tiny egg inside the ovaries of our developing mothers while they were still babies inside the wombs of our grandmothers.

The emerging field of epigenetics is starting to connect those dots and look at the ways we store information about the environment in how our genes are expressed. We may have perfect genetic material, but it is not being fully expressed because of the ways in which the epigenetic information from the environment is acting upon it. The gene could still be there and have the correctly-coded instructions for making a healthy protein, but there is a big red flag posted next to it that says not to turn it on, or that it is not safe to turn it on fully right now. Conversely, you may carry a variation of a gene that has been identified with a certain disease, but this gene may not be expressed unless the same or similar stressors exist in this generation. We were taught that the nucleus of the cell that holds the DNA is giving all of the directions, when really the cell membrane has an important role in determining the safety of the exterior that drives survival. The field of epigenetics is working at that intersection of genes and environment and teaching us about how our ancestors pass down important information about survival. Sometimes, that information is very specifically tuned to something that happened generations ago and doesn't apply to the physical or social environment that we live in now.

If this all sounds fascinating, then I encourage you to keep exploring and keep learning. But if it sounds intimidating or complicated or even irrelevant, then just know that your earliest experiences matter. For too long the medical authorities have been telling the mothers not to trust their intuition. They have been telling us not to trust the wisdom of our grandmothers. The authorities tried to tell the mothers that what happens during birth doesn't matter because babies can't feel anything and can't remember. But the mothers have always known that this is just not true. How your grandmother and your mother were treated and how they felt physically and emotionally during their births still matters; regardless of how many years may have passed. The scientists are learning to pay more attention to the ways in which babies store those early memories. The healers are learning about the powerful effects of the birth stories that are still held by our bodies because they were never given voice, and never allowed to heal. These unexpressed fears manifest as physical symptoms.

When researchers study these patterns at the

population level, they can see whether the correlations are statistically significant. But if you just start to think about it, you can see some of these connections for yourself. For example, imagine that coworker who is always getting to the office late. She drives you a little crazy, because she just hates to be rushed, even if everyone else is waiting for her. Perhaps she is really just still upset at a subconscious level about having had her mother's labor induced. Was she forced to be born before she was ready? Now that she is an adult, she insists on showing up on her own schedule. But if always letting her friends and coworkers down is starting to impact her relationships, maybe it is time to let that old story go and create room to form a new habit. There are other examples of how we continue to carry these early memories, even into adulthood. Some babies who are born with a forceps-assisted birth may still feel pain in a ring around their head when they feel stressed. When we look at the patterns and bring those unrecognized stories out into the light then they can finally be processed. When we give voice to their truth, the memories can finally be filed away as past events by the psyche, and real healing can begin.

Giving voice to those stories is further complicated by the fact that those earliest memories are not remembered in the same way that we think of memory. After we reach the age when we are aware of the days of the week and the hours of the day and we are verbally narrating our stories and beginning to write words and sentences to describe our world, then we start to catalog our memories in linear and structured ways. If we are asked to share about something that we did, like when we sit down to dinner and ask everyone what they did today, we have a timeline and a narrative to describe our experiences. But, when we are babies, our memories are not stored in words and in categories; they are stored as feelings deep in our muscle tissues and in the fascia that binds all of our internal organs together and in the energy centers of our bodies. We come equipped with genetic instructions from our ancestors, but we use those foundational early experiences to wire our biochemistry and establish the settings for what we call our gut reactions as we are attuned to the current environment of our infancy.

If you are like me, maybe you think of your memories as a recording of your experiences, a database of files, or a bookshelf with your stories neatly catalogued. Maybe the memories are arranged by year or alphabetically. I know I store things like names alphabetically because when I'm trying to remember one, my mind works in slow motion, laboriously searching through files. First I go find the cabinet with the first letter of the name, then pull out the drawer with the right number of syllables, then I can finally get to where I stored the detail. Usually though, it's too much pressure to remember the name when I'm put on the spot and then it will just pop into my head long after whoever asked me has walked away. My mind continued the search subconsciously, spitting out the answer later, long after I was aware that I even wanted that information. I feel like this was a bad system for my brain to set up though, because it is not very efficient or useful. I find that little kids often pronounce names better than adults because they are not tied down to trying to spell it and store the information somewhere. When you tell a child your name, they not only believe you (unlike the adults who want to tell you that you must be saying it wrong because it's not matching something in their memory bank), they just say it back to you and then remember the feel of it on their tongue or the music of the name. They might file it with a picture of your face and a memory of where they were when they first met you. This must be why we do really well with those names that we are familiar with from before we learned to write and the newer ones bother us a bit. Adults start to panic when something is new and different. While adults try to quickly figure out where to file the information into their memory, they loop back to the conversation and find that they've lost the pronunciation and can't echo it back to you.

This is why I try to chat with babies and toddlers as much as possible, because it is a treat to talk to them before they've lost that innate wisdom. I find that at about three years old, toddlers have enough words for a really interesting conversation but they are still quite connected to their spirit and to the universe. This is when you can get the best stories and learn some really important things if you respect these small teachers. Sadly, if you are paying close attention and really listening, by age six or seven you can start to see that they are worrying because they notice that they are starting to forget some of that wisdom.

Mind vs Body is another thing that we like to compartmentalize in the western world. When we try to put things neatly into their own separate compartments, I think we lose a little of each. We end up with adults who are hyper-aware of their medical symptoms, seeking healthcare, but with no real awareness of their underlying feelings. When our heads are so disconnected from our bodies, we miss all the whispers of information that our body is trying to tell us something. We wait until our body is screaming in pain before we start to pay attention to it. If we learned to tune in and listen to our body's innate wisdom in the same way that we listen to those little children, then we could prevent disease and promote health and not need to be cured or rescued.

If you look at a graph of where we choose to spend our healthcare dollars, it is evidence of how our culture has its pyramid upside down and balancing on its tip instead of firmly planted on a wide base of support. We should spend our resources of time and energy and money on primary prevention like community programs, promoting healthy families, and protecting our vulnerable populations. Secondary prevention includes all of our screening programs to find the signs of disease in early stages when it is easy to treat, and gathering statistics to see the patterns and be able to recognize who most needs our help. Instead, we cut funding to primary and secondary prevention, and spend it on tertiary care which is only meant to save the ones who fell through the safety net or slipped through the cracks. We have created a system where we wait until people are sick and then offer elaborate procedures, expensive medications, and life-saving surgeries. Instead of being proactive and efficient with our resources by preserving and promoting health, we build huge medical centers to care for the sick and create a lot of jobs in healthcare.

When I started studying health, I wanted to save the world. Ever since I was a little girl, I have been very spiritual. I wanted to be a nun and a teacher and a writer and a scientist. However, above all else, I wanted to be a mother. My teachers and my guidance counselors told me that I had to choose just one path. I was told that I couldn't have a career and raise a family. But I knew that I couldn't really choose just one of my passions. Even starting with choosing a major in college was a hard enough decision. Then life happens, and the path seems to choose you.

After my favorite cousin died from a strange virus, I began studying microbiology, virology, and epidemiology. I didn't want other families to go through what my family had. I was taught to look for the root cause of disease. I studied global health and looked at the patterns of disease in populations. I conducted my research in the field and in the lab, and I started my career. I was already breaking society's rules by refusing to check off only a single box and I became a certified teacher at the same time that I studied science. As a teacher, I started a program with an integrated multidisciplinary curriculum for high school students, so that we could read about the poetry of science and be inspired to take action. I taught my students to see the intricate patterns and the interconnectedness and beauty of all the aspects of life. We explored the similarities between the way that systems work in organisms and in organizations. We discussed the philosophy that the whole Earth lives and breathes as one organism. It is all interconnected.

I knew that to save the world, or at least to play my part in reducing some of the suffering, promoting health by working with mothers and babies was the most efficient and effective way to affect change. It's not like I invented the idea myself though. There are models in public health that show how you can just look at the numbers for maternal and infant mortality and from that handful of statistics you will know everything about the health of that population. In most places in the world, the statistics show a direct correlation to how much money the government has available to spend on their people. For all the money that we spend on healthcare in America, the outcomes for women and children's health are simply embarrassing. We have enough money, it is just not being used to pay for what matters. Preventative measures like proper nutrition and healthy home environments are a better long-term investment than emergency room visits.

It wasn't until I became a mother myself that these numbers and these issues became much more real, and much more important. All of those scientific concepts that I knew academically about biochemistry could not have prepared me for the reality of feeling the personality changes that come over you from the cocktail of pregnancy hormones. And nothing that I had read in my science books about how we create memories could have prepared me for the fact that it was not just my own repressed memories but those of my ancestors that could surface during profound moments in life. This reality surfaced when I had my first vaginal birth and ancestral memories all came flooding back, as if they were my very own. The environmental health classes that I had taken did not explain how strongly one could be triggered by something as simple as a smell or a taste or a sound. The senses that may have meant "danger" generations ago suddenly thrust you into a full blown fight-or-flight-response faster than you can say intergenerational family trauma.

Our earliest memories are stored in our bodies in the first energy center, the root chakra; our base. There is a large muscle called the psoas that connects our spine to our legs and helps us to stand upright. (2) If we feel connected and have a strong base of support, then we can stand firm in our beliefs. When we feel unsure of our standing in the world or if we feel like the rug is pulled out from under us, or if our world has been shaken, then our psoas tightens and we start to experience physical pain. Because this muscle connects in so many places it can cause pain in the hips, knees, back and can cause pelvic and menstrual pain.

This is just one example of how our emotional health impacts our physical health. When someone tells us to just grow a spine, we know that we have not been standing up for ourselves. In families where we feel that sense of being spineless maybe we also have a story about how everyone in our family has a bad back. We expect it and we're used to it, so we don't even look for ways to heal it. Noticing those cultural sayings that we use to express how we feel about not being supported also gives us clues to why they cause those painful symptoms in our bodies.

The psoas is also said to link all the way from our pelvic root to our limbic system in the brain. (2) The limbic system is also called our primitive brain and it contains all of the basic instincts for survival like our fight/flight/freeze response to signs of danger. It can and does override all higher thinking, survival comes first. As mammals, we have many survival instincts that kick in when we are giving birth, because we are never in more danger than when we are allowing ourselves to become vulnerable enough to do such powerful work.

When we are babies, we are not really able to fight back and we are not capable of standing up for ourselves or running away. Instead, we use the only tools that are available to us. Many babies learn to dissociate/ tune out/play dead when they are not protected and nurtured in those early months or years. Just like when you see a spider or a snake, you've suddenly raised your awareness of every single thing that moves. Children who do not feel safe establish a hyper-vigilance as their baseline state of being. The problem then becomes that we stay in that aroused state when we are operating in survival mode. Our body is misreading cues from the physical environment and conserving resources to be able to fight back or run away at any second. It is not sending any energy to other important functions like growth or learning. In that state of survival, we slow down digestion, turn off our immunity, and dial down our reproductive capabilities.

This is where the science is finally catching up to what the grandmothers have been telling us all along, that if we help the mothers to feel safe and supported during the pregnancy, birth and postpartum period, then we can help the newest generations create better opportunities to wire themselves for health instead of setting the dial to emergency mode. If the world does not seem safe, then those resources are sent to the defense systems for a quick burn lasting maybe only 30-50 years, compared to when the baby is relaxed and prepares to budget its energy efficiently, save for the future and make those resources last for a long and healthy life of maybe closer to 100 years.

Over the last few centuries, the medicalization of childbirth has waged a widespread war on families by breaking that instinctive bond between mothers and babies that is so important to survival. Some of the resulting attachment disorders could be traced back to the use of medical interventions in healthy childbirth. Whole generations of children were operating in emergency-mode, and as they reached adulthood we started to see epidemics of diseases that are caused by chronic stress and trauma. Our bodies are beautifully and wonderfully made with intricate systems made to handle moments of intense stress. We have probably all heard at least one story of someone who was blessed with super-speed to run away from that dog or jump out from in front of the train or superhuman strength to lift the car off of their baby. Our bodies store those amazing reserves of energy for just those moments and can mobilize instantly, sending signals to our muscles faster than our brains can even notice it happen. And after that amazing response, we are supposed to then shake it off and calm back down and resume our normal operating procedure. We are then able to build up our reserves again. When you are not able to complete that stress-response cycle and come back to baseline, it is called trauma.

We often think of the big dramatic moment as the trauma, but it is really the body staying in an activated state for too long that classifies the incident as a trauma, no matter how big or small the stressor may seem. Sometimes we recognize it as significant, like that time we got in a car accident, or it could have been something seemingly unimportant, like realizing that our fly was down and thinking that everyone was laughing at us the whole time. We keep replaying the day in our minds. The details of that stressful moment are often stored as a traumatic memory and we put up red flags around each of those facts. To our bodies, the event stays "in the present," it is never over and done, it is still happening. Now every time you see a blue car, your body remembers and prepares, sometimes even before you realize that you've seen it. Maybe you check the zipper on your jeans three times before leaving the restroom now. In our stressful modern culture, surrounded by constant warnings about all of the possible dangers from friends and TV and social media, we tend to stay in that activated state all of the time. And when we are always ready to fight or run away we are not sending any energy to our digestion or reproduction or immunity. Our bodies are not saving any resources for the future because that is too uncertain. Our lives are in reality so much safer than when we lived in caves or in small families trying to survive alone out on the prairie, but we live in constant fear of all the unknown and invisible dangers. When you are stressed-out all of the time, you are also not capable of learning or making long term plans which is why so many of these babies whose biochemical pathways were wired for stress start to really have noticeable trouble when they start school.

While I was preparing for the births of my babies, I learned so much about the energy blocks in the root chakra and how it contributed to the symptoms that I was experiencing. As I worked on letting go of the stories that no longer served me, I learned more and more about the connections to my family stories. My mom was also doing a lot of her own exploration and she found the courage to ask my grandmother more about her own childhood. My mother had always known that she had to have surgery on her eyes when she was a baby because she had been almost blind when she was born. But what she hadn't ever realized was that they had kept her in isolation for two weeks. At that time, the doctors were so concerned about the risk of infections that they did not even allow the baby's own mother to touch them. My grandmother was listening to the medical advice about what was best for her baby even though her heart was breaking from the separation. My mother had her infant body strapped down so that she would not pull at the bandages. With her eyes covered she had no way of knowing that my grandmother was so close and that she visited every day, and the thick glass window kept her from hearing her mother's voice.

After that traumatic early separation, it was no surprise that my infant mother had attachment issues and failed to thrive. My grandmother tried so hard to be a good mom but the doctors had no advice to give her when her baby wouldn't nurse or take a bottle. My grandmother used to tell me a story about when she was grocery shopping one day, carrying this twenty pound baby in her arms, and then a woman gasped out loud in shock when she put her down on the floor to walk. She looked like a newborn but was almost three years old at the time. In addition to having trouble gaining weight, she was often sick. When my mother started going to school she was sick so often, sometimes missing school almost the entire winter, so she always fell behind in her lessons and never felt included in the activities of the other schoolchildren.

As a new mom myself, I was really able to connect to this story and understand my mom better than ever and see how the medical trauma had broken the bond between my mother and my grandmother. When my siblings and I were babies, my mother was determined to hold us close and nurse us throughout our infancy. But despite all of her wishes for natural birth and parenting, they gave her a mixture of Morphine and Scopolamine at her first birth which put her into what they call "twilight sleep," which robbed her of her memories and left her angry and feeling violated. They also used Pitocin for the contractions but that made it harder for her baby to bond. My brother weaned early and pushed her away. She was hurting and exhausted and feeling like she sucked at mothering when she found out that she was pregnant with me.

She tells me about how my birth was so healing for her. She refused to let them near her with any medication, and then because I didn't have to work those drugs out of my system, I was an easier baby and she began to believe that she could be a good mother after all. She went on to have three more babies. I'm glad that it worked out the way that it did because I can't even picture my world without my brothers and sister in it.

My father's infancy was not easy either and he also had a few instances of early medical trauma. His mother didn't have him until she was older and she went to a healer to seek help when she couldn't conceive. Both my paternal grandmother and grandfather lived into their eighties, but they both died before I was ever born and I never got to meet them. I didn't get to grow up hearing that grandmother tell stories at the kitchen table, but my father's sister told me about her and it was nice to hear about the ways in which I act like her sometimes. One time, I actually got to hear my dad's mother telling stories when we listened to some old reel-to-reel tapes that she had sent to my father when he was serving overseas. He didn't have many tapes left because at the time he would listen to what she had sent and then record over it with his news and mail it back to her. I felt lucky to have that one tape and I sat and listened to her just telling him stories about what was going on in the neighborhood and I felt like she was talking to me while putting cookies into the oven while I helped her in the kitchen.

I've heard the stories about how my father's conception was a miracle and I've heard about all the miraculous things that happened when he was born. He was premature and he was one of the tiniest babies they'd ever had at that hospital. He made it into some medical journals because of the techniques they used to keep him alive that had never been used before. He tells me about how he was baptized three times because they didn't think that he would live. The nurse baptized him quickly after the birth because nobody expected him to survive the first hour. When the priest got to the hospital and my father was still alive, he baptized him too. Then, when he actually survived long enough to be brought home from the hospital, they had a christening at the church with the family present. So it all makes for great stories, and obviously he lived long enough to become a father himself, but I often wonder about the effects of all of those procedures on that tiny baby. You have to give them credit for all the effort that they made to care for his soul, but nobody knew how to remove the effects of the trauma from his little body.

They use needle sticks as a measure of pain in infants when they do studies on the stress and trauma of Neonatal Intensive Care Unit stays for premature babies. But in those days many doctors actually believed that babies couldn't feel pain, so many procedures were performed without any painkillers or anesthesia. My mother said that even into adulthood my father would wake with nightmares as his mind and body remembered some of the procedures. So even when we're talking about life-saving measures and we know that the medical staff was doing everything that they could to keep him alive, the body still remembers the pain and the trauma.

Some of the reasons why certain experiences are classified as traumatic are because there is something dangerous or stressful and there is nothing that you can do. You can't make it stop. You can't run away. You can't fight back. As infants, we literally put our lives in our caregivers' hands and we are too small to fight back and can't get up and leave. So babies tend to dissociate, check out, and have their spirit leave their body until they feel safe to return. Sometimes they are actually called "good babies" because they don't cry, but you can tell when their stillness and blank stare is indicating that they have given up on expecting help to come. This is what we call freezing, and it is a great tool for survival when you can't use either the fight or flight response. As we learn to recognize the significance of these trauma responses, we will be even more aware of these silent cries for help.

As adults we often find ourselves in similar situations. We are physically more capable of getting up and leaving the room than an infant, but often social conditioning keeps us stuck. Maybe you can't leave that job that you hate because you need the paycheck, so you don't fight the boss, you don't run away, you just keep going day after day, but you do the minimum and are not really giving it your all. Maybe you are afraid but you know that it is safer to appease your abuser than to fight back. Maybe you need a painful procedure, but you stay in that dentist's chair because you believe that it is best, so you fight your urge to run away. Each of those moments when your body is in the stress response but you can't act on it, the feeling is stored in your body as a trauma and needs to find a way to be released after the moment has passed. Animals are really good at shaking it off after that rush of stress hormones takes over in the fight or flight response. Once they are safe, they twitch and shudder and shake the trauma out of their physical bodies. They might remember the important details about the danger signs for next time, but then they bring their energy and awareness back into the present moment. We are told to ignore those instincts, to just get over it, to forget it and to act like everything is fine. We just keep going through the motions of getting back to normal, but our bodies remember.

As I researched more about Scopolamine and how it was used in hospital births during the era of "twilight sleep," I was shocked about what I read. It is the same drug that they use as a truth serum for interrogations because it makes the subject very compliant. The women would stay conscious in the sense that they could move their body as they were instructed and could even answer questions, but they were not aware of what they were doing and they formed no conscious memories of what happened during that time. The passive submission was useful for the doctors, but the women would not labor well (in that the contractions were not pushing the baby down and out) so they often would cut a significant episiotomy in the woman's perineum and then pull the baby out with large metal forceps. The women would wake up with no memory of labor or childbirth and after close to a week of separation, they would be sent home with a new baby. They had no way of knowing why looking at their beautiful baby made them feel sad or angry or powerless. (3)

The partners and family were not allowed at the birth because it was too hard to watch as the woman sometimes turned into a raging monster that had to be tied to the bed. (3) It was hard enough for the nurses to have to see, and that is where we get most of the eyewitness accounts. But the family had no idea what was really going on behind those doors. Early in the twentieth century, many doctors who saw the effects of this drug asked that its use be discontinued. It's interesting to read the history because it actually had become a women's rights issue. Mothers were telling their friends to request medicated birth because they were tired of being told that women have to suffer through the pain of childbirth to pay for Eve's sin in the garden. They were trying to end one form of oppression but didn't have any way of knowing that it was just a new form of torture. As I read the accounts of what birth was like during "twilight sleep," I pieced it together with what I've learned about trauma and realized how dangerous this practice really was. There is a big difference between how trauma is stored by a baby and by someone older who can associate a memory of a traumatic event with the pain that they are experiencing. If you hurt yourself in an accident, you know why you are in pain, and while you still need to physically recover you need not be afraid that this will become a regular occurrence. You still may jump awake in the middle of the night as the memories of the accident come back, but then you learn to tell yourself that it was in the past. You put up red flags around all those details in the story and you get anxious when you have to drive the car on a rainy night again. But at least your logical brain remembers and you know why your pulse is racing and your palms are sweaty.

With the era of "twilight sleep," I feel like so many women were sent home with their new baby along with the physical and emotional effects of trauma, but with no memory of why they were feeling these things. As if having a newborn to take care of all day and night is not hard enough, these women would wake up from their precious moments of sleep shaking and sweating or even screaming from the nightmares. And many women felt like they were handed a stranger and forced to go work 24-7 caring for a being they had no emotional connection to because they were robbed of that vital period of early bonding in those hours right after birth. And despite searching, I have not really been able to find any specific research on the long-term health effects of this traumatic break in the mother/baby bond, but I have a feeling that amongst other things it would have a biochemical effect on their stress-response.

Despite the recommendations to stop using the drug in 1905, doctors continued to use scopolamine in labor well into the 1970s. (3) I am not surprised that the babies that were born during this time period are now suffering from diabetes, obesity, cardiovascular disease and other chronic diseases that are associated with stress. (5) At an early age, their biochemistry was wired for a stressful environment by their early medical trauma, and then they were sent home with mothers that were in no shape to give them the nurturing that would have healed them. There are actually studies that show the healing power of hugs. There are also laboratory studies with rats where they can place a previously traumatized pup into a cage with a nurturing mother and the loving touch will rewire their biochemical and neural pathways. (5, 6) It is so good to know that we *can* heal, and that there are simple (and free) solutions like hugs and loving touch.

I can't help but be angry when I think about those doctors and nurses, who knew why the fathers weren't allowed into the maternity ward (because they didn't want them to see their wives grunting like animals and thrashing against the restraints that held them to the bed,) but continued to administer those drugs to mothers and babies for decades. We are trained to respect authority, and it is hard to break out of those patterns. We follow orders and we follow procedures. I am sure that many of those doctors and nurses were wonderful people, and that they had to go against their gut instincts to keep their jobs. And the families were most likely operating on the belief that the doctor knows best, and might have been told that the mother or baby needed saving. Sometimes we come home from the hospital with wounds and scars, but we believe that the benefits outweigh the risks. So even though it is hard, we need to put ourselves in their shoes and understand how even when women went home bruised and battered and sometimes had torn the skin off of their arms from pulling at the straps, they were not able to speak up or say "no" to the medical community.

Over time and with more perspective though, women started to demand more. I am glad that my mother's generation paved the way for my generation to bring natural births and homebirths back into the picture. When someone talks about the natural birth movement and makes it seem like women were fighting over something trivial, like wanting pretty wallpaper in the rooms where they gave birth, ask them how they feel about "twilight sleep."

While I was searching for answers about "twilight sleep," I actually started to feel more and more physical pain as my body raised those red flags. It was as if my body was anticipating a healing, a discharge of the traumatic energy. All that emotional pain that I was carrying for my mother and my grandmother started to present itself in my lower back and my hips until I could literally feel it in my bones. When it got harder and harder to walk, I finally broke down and made an appointment with my friend who uses a technique called Myofascial Release as part of her physical therapy services. She told me that she finds the block where the energy is stuck in your fascia and she holds that spot with deep pressure until she feels the energy flowing again. I personally think that she uses her intuition as much as she uses her hands to find the blockage. As I lay on the table while she released the pain and restored health to my fascia, I actually started to see some images flow behind my closed eyelids. The women of my family would each come to mind one at a time and I saw these big ugly caterpillars wiggle out of my abdomen. Then they grew wings and beautiful butterflies flew up and away.

As the subconscious memories start to be released from your tissue and enter your consciousness, your body can store them as a cognitive memory. Then the old trauma can finally be filed away as something that happened in the past, and you no longer need to keep feeling it in the present. The danger signs can still be stored as useful information, but they no longer need to trigger you into a full blown stress response. After you release the trauma but retain the learning in your epigenetics for future generations, they will be able to have healthy responses to environmental clues. When you see movement out of the corner of your eye, you can calmly see that it is just a cat and not a tiger, and quickly bring your heart rate back to normal. When we are carrying around too many old traumas, we are constantly in an elevated state of alert and alarm and we use too much energy to stay on guard and don't have enough left for our current needs like digestion and immunity.

If you are looking for a Myofascial Release practitioner in your area, make sure that you find one that will be able to hold space for you (if you are like

me and you need to let yourself shake and sob all the
way through the emotional release until you get to the
healing) and not just someone who learned the physical
techniques. That discharge is normal and natural and
necessary and you need someone who understands that
important aspect of this work of trauma clearing that
leads to physical healing. You can call the practitioner
for a quick consultation first and ask them about their
training, and also ask them about how much time they
devote to each client. Sessions should be at least an
hour and they should give you some time after that
before the next client is scheduled so they can help you
to process anything that comes up during the physical
part of the session.

Even if you have to pay out of pocket for the better
practitioner, it is so worth it to give it the time to really
let that old trauma go. You don't even need to know
what the trauma was, you just need to feel that it is
coming up in your symptoms and you know that it
is time to give it some attention. After I gave myself
permission to push through my cultural training of
feeling embarrassment and my fear of making myself
vulnerable, I was able to get up and walk away pain
free in under an hour! I no longer listen when someone
suggests staying in bed for two weeks when I throw

my back out. I just schedule a session with her and heal the root cause of why I hurt myself in the first place. I used to feel guilty about spending the money on myself, even when I was really in a lot of pain. I felt like I was taking money out of my family budget to treat myself. I felt like I should just suffer through it. I had to realize that I am the center of this family and that I take care of everyone else, so taking care of me is actually taking care of the whole family. And I am laying the foundation for the next generation by modeling this for my children. They look up to me, so I need to set a good example. I picture my daughter saying that she should suffer and be in pain and that she doesn't need to bother anyone by asking for help, and I think of how ridiculous that sounds. Of course she deserves to walk without being in pain, and I guess that means that I do, too.

We often marvel at the transformation of the caterpillar into the butterfly, but the first transition actually starts with the egg. Embryology is the fascinating science of that transformation from a single cell to a complex multicellular organism. You could spend an entire career studying how eggs on the sunnier side of the leaf thrive while others struggle to survive. You can study how in years when the temperature is lower, the pattern on the butterfly wings actually includes thicker black stripes so that they can warm themselves more easily. (7) Humans go through an amazing embryonic stage just like those caterpillars the turn into butterflies, but we transform from a little squiggly thing into a complicated individual in the darkness and quiet of the womb. We are wonderfully and beautifully made.

Even Jesus taught about environmental health in his parables when he described the seed that falls on good soil and has all of the nurturing that it needs to grow verses the seed that falls on rock and fails to thrive. (8) Maybe they had good DNA, were planted in rich soil and had the perfect temperature and just the right amount of sun and water, but then they have weeds that grow up around them and choke them. You can use this parable to think about nature vs. nurture, genes vs. environment, and how our thoughts and our emotional health impact our physical health. The butterfly is often used as a symbol of transformation, and you can use that imagery as you think about what changes you are ready to make in your life. Where are you letting your guilt or shame hold you back? Where do you feel pain in your body when you read this? Whose pain are you carrying? Which family stories are you holding in your root?

Things to think about:

- What makes you feel at home? What are your favorite comfort foods? What are your favorite scents? Where do you feel safe? Visualize somewhere that you feel totally at home.

- Have you asked your mother or grandmother to tell their birth story? What were your earliest experiences like? What was the socio-cultural climate like when you were born?

- What are some of the big stories that your family tells? How have those shaped your life?

- If you have given birth, which birth stories did you hear growing up that impacted your birth? What are your beliefs around birth? Where did those come from?

- How do you handle stress? Do you have any physical side effects that seem related to how your body reacts to chronic stress? Is your life stressful every day?

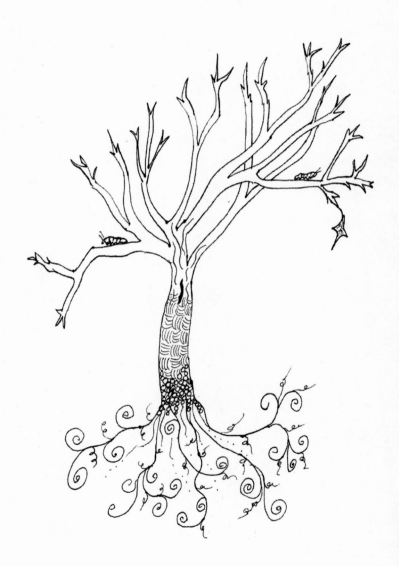

Chapter 2: Seeds of Self-Worth

Our first energy center is our root and it holds all of our earliest body memories of how safe and protected we feel in the world. As we crawl into our second year of life outside the womb, we start to explore our surroundings and our creativity. This year is focused on feelings, and is when we start to make words and see how much power we have. As we learn to move away and explore and start to gain the sense that we can exist separately from our mothers, we still tend to test the security of the attachment. About halfway through that second year, many experience some separation anxiety and would rather be with their parents or primary caregivers than with strangers. With healthy attachment, we can learn to trust that even if someone leaves, they will always come back.

This is also the stage at which we start to learn more about our bodies as we learn to walk around, feed ourselves and start potty-training. Many people find that they have stored feelings of shame in this energy center, in their sexual and reproductive organs, bladder and intestines. In cultures where your sex and your gender define you and determine your opportunities, it can be especially hard to send healthy energy to this area. Many times, we learn to be ashamed of our bodily functions before we even learn about all of the amazing things that our bodies can do.

We store feelings about our value, our power and our ability to have some control over our surroundings in that second energy center. As we grow older, whenever we have feelings that trigger our emotions about our self-worth, like financial issues or feelings of being in control, they are stored in this energy center. If we hold too much guilt or blame and shame in this center, this chakra can become blocked. This is also the center of our creativity, and if we have projects that we are called to do, but cannot bring them to fruition for some reason and our creative force is suppressed, this energy center can be blocked.

Finances can become entwined with creativity when we have ideas of what we want to accomplish in the world, but feel stuck economically. I have been teaching my children about finances since they were small. We talk a lot about saving, and when they get money in their birthday card they put it away and save it for something important instead of spending it right away on candy. When we are at the concession stand at the baseball game and it costs $4 for one ice cream, we talk about how we can buy a box with enough ice cream for all of us on the way home for $3. We wait a little longer, everyone is happy, and we save for the future. (I also make sure to pack other snacks for the game because at some ages delayed gratification doesn't really work that well.) I know which stores have the better prices and I try to play it smart with finances so that they can have the money when those bigger opportunities come up.

When talking to another mom on the playground about my strategy, I called it my "Little No for the Big Yes" plan, because when I say "no" to the little things that they don't really need, later we have the money to take them all the amusement park. I tell them to save their birthday money so that when they are in high school they can go on the Paris trip. To be able to save for the future, you need to trust and believe that it will come. You need to have some base of security before you can do any financial planning. I try my best to teach them how to find a healthy combination of planning for the future, believing you are worth good things, and also getting that ice cream and enjoying the moment. As I tried to model all of that for my kids, I started to see so many ways in which I communicated to them that I wasn't really able to see my own worth.

For many women who are raised in a patriarchal culture, our sense of self is tied so strongly to people that drain us instead of build us up. Our worth is often determined in relation to how others can use our bodies, not in our own creativity and power. We grow up surrounded by images that use women's bodies to market and sell everything from tires to toilet paper. The beauty of a woman adds value to any product; but she is never given any of the actual credit when she is treated like an accessory. For the most part, the women do the important work of feeding and teaching and caring for the children, but are not given enough compensation or respect. It is no wonder that these messages get internalized and so many women have blocks in the flow of energy through their second energy center. These blocks can result in symptoms including painful periods and irregular menstrual cycles, bladder infections and cervical cancers. In these patriarchal patterns women are not given enough credit for their creations, for their work, for their art and their contributions to society. Even when they miraculously grow entire humans in their womb they are not given enough credit. And if a woman chooses not to become a mother or can't have children, she is shamed, sometimes cast aside or triggered by constant questions and comments on the subject. When we get caught up in these power dynamics we tend to determine a person's worth by what they can do for others. When we fall into this trap we end up feeling like we will never be enough.

At this time I was home with a newborn, a preschooler and two kindergarteners, I read a lot of children's books from the library. One of the kids brought home a book about butterflies, and although we use them as symbols of change, hope and life and we love to put pictures of them on everything, I was surprised to learn just how little I knew about them. I don't know about you, but I love how much I can learn from a children's book. I tried to search for the book again and I didn't find it on the shelf at the library or in my internet search, but there were a few facts that got stuck in my head. They kept replaying long after we had returned the book. Between the beautiful pictures and the concise messages, they really can leave an impression on you. Even after studying biology for years in school, a science book for kids still had more to teach me.

Snuggling up and reading this book with my kids made me think about how we need to be more like the caterpillar, always looking to grow and change. I never realized that the caterpillar has to grow a new exoskeleton five times before it is even ready to transform into a butterfly. We go through something like that as we become mothers. We grow and change throughout the months of our pregnancy or an adoption process which sometimes takes even longer. We know that we are mothers and we feel ourselves changing and we are so in love with our babies and the idea of being their mother, but we are still not fully in the parenting role yet. While we are expecting, we can still act somewhat as an individual and have some semblance of our old life for a little bit longer.

The caterpillar grows the new exoskeleton inside the old one and keeps it safe until it is ready and then it molts the old one, shedding it, letting it go. Then it eats it, because that was a lot of hard work and they need to recycle those vital nutrients. I'd never really understood those cultures in which women eat their placentas. Even though this trend was starting to be resurrected in a new westernized version, in which it is dried and encapsulated in pills, I had always just dismissed the thought as too "out there." We like the idea of the placenta and we have jewelry with the tree of life symbol on it, but we don't like to remember that it is a biological, in the flesh, and very real thing that gives us life. We also prefer to think of the butterflies as a symbol and when we get too into the details they start to seem more like creatures. One time I went to a butterfly conservatory and when one landed on my shoulder I looked over at it and looked it right in the face and I never realized how creepy they were up close. Despite being a biology-lover, I guess I prefer to watch these insects flitting about from flower to flower. I like the distance and the perspective that it gives me.

So, using my butterfly symbolically instead of realistically, I will think about how on my journey to becoming Magdalena, I need to go through the stages of change as I transform into my new self. This butterfly book had helped me to realize that it is okay to have to go through many stages before being able to spread my wings and fly. I had always thought that the caterpillar just ate and grew for a season, wrapped itself in a cocoon, and then came out a butterfly. I had never broken it down into all of those steps before. I didn't know that the caterpillar repeated that growing stage five times before even making the cocoon. Although I found the message in an unexpected place, this children's book had given me permission to take my time and to be gentle with myself. I knew that I needed to stop, reflect, gather my strength, and get some rest between each stage of my journey.

There is another really great children's book called "The Caterpillar and the Pollywog." (11) Maybe you like frogs better than butterflies and this can be your symbol. In this story the tadpole is amazed as the caterpillar tells him about her upcoming transformation and he is mesmerized as he watches her wrap herself in her cocoon. He waits with anticipation for her to emerge in all her beauty and he's so entranced that he doesn't even realize that he is going through his own metamorphosis. Then, when she comes out of the cocoon, she tells him how different he looks. When he looks down at himself he realizes that he has grown legs and become a frog. Sometimes when we are so focused on how amazing everyone else is, we forget to recognize our own power and our own growth. Maybe the dads can use the frog as their symbol for the changes that come with fatherhood.

When you crouch down and look at the world through the eyes of your child you can discover so many things that you never noticed in your own childhood, while you were so busy worrying about growing and changing into an adult. I find myself telling them to slow down and appreciate what they have now, but they don't. None of us can. But maybe we adults are the ones who are meant to appreciate childhood by walking it again, alongside our kids. I am looking forward to even more of these insights and opportunities when I become a grandmother and I have even more time for reflection and appreciation. Mothers, and even more so grandmothers, are so full of wisdom that nobody seems to hear. Maybe the teachings are for us and not for the children after all. I'm certainly not the only one who has figured out that our children teach us far more than we'll ever teach them.

As my children grew and changed before my eyes, I was constantly in awe and gratitude. I started to feel a

SEEDS OF SELF-WORTH

new sense of worth in myself as I knew that they were so healthy and happy because of how I had literally let myself be transformed to bring them into this world. I had carried the twins first and my whole body needed to adjust to make room for them to grow. Some people say silly things like how you "get two for the price of one." Those people do not know what it feels like as the bones in your ribcage slowly move back into their previous position for six months or so after the birth. They don't know how it feels when your pelvis separates and your organs move out of the way. It was so much more comfortable to have one baby grow in my belly then to have two pushing my bones out of the way to make more room.

And I think of all the women who put all cares for themselves aside and let their bodies be cut open because they would do anything for their babies. There are so many shows about surgeons on TV now that surgery seems so commonplace and ordinary that we don't even stop to think about how huge of a sacrifice these mothers are making when they say "yes" to major abdominal surgery and all of the physical and emotional implications of having a surgical birth. After the surgeon performs a cesarean section, not only does the new mother have to recover from major surgery while caring for a new baby, she has to live with all of the implications of that choice. She is often not only managing the physical pains of recovery, she is trying to figure out why she may feel like she is grieving. She may feel like she missed out on something or that her body failed her. She may wonder if she made the right choice. Or she may not have been given a choice, and she feels powerless. There may have been coercion or the illusion of choice, and she feels cheated or used. When everyone is telling her that it is okay, she wonders why she doesn't feel "fine." She feels like she is lying every time that she smiles and says that she is "fine." She doesn't know how to just keep going and pretending that this isn't huge. She may have trouble bonding with the baby when the memory of the traumatic birth is associated with the child that she loves. There are so many cultural beliefs that women have internalized about their bodies and about themselves as mothers, and she can't just "get over it" when she feels like her body failed her and she is not a good enough mother. This moment matters, and mothers need to have their voices heard and their fears and their grief acknowledged and they need to be able to stand fully in their power as they make this important choice.

Typically when the woman is in labor and it

comes time to make this choice to say "yes" to having this major surgery performed, the anesthesiologists and obstetricians barely even need to pause and wait for an answer because they know that mothers will automatically put their baby's life before their own. But it is not okay that they have stopped even asking the question. They have stopped pausing long enough to give the mother enough information for her to choose to give informed consent. We need to honor the sacrifice. We need to be respectful of the mothers and not just push them aside to get to the baby. While we are in awe of the miracle of the baby that has grown out of virtually nothing into someone unique, and special, and new. We need to also acknowledge the beauty that lies in the transformation of the woman into a new mother (or new kind of a mother if this is not her first birth). We need to pause in this moment and let her give voice to her concerns, and let her stand in her power and make the choice. The cesarean scar that the woman wears right across her second energy center should add to her worth, not make her feel broken. Like stretch marks that show that you are a mother and not a young girl anymore, a cesarean scar is not a sign of failure; it is a badge of courage.

I didn't grow up with high self-esteem, but as a

mother I was in awe of what my body was capable of and I wanted to scream it from the rooftops. But we are taught that girls can't brag about their accomplishments. We are taught in unspoken ways to look down and bat our eyes and act as if it was nothing. We are made to feel in so many ways that it will hurt someone else if we lay claim to our own awesomeness. With time I have learned that when you actually take ownership of your own success, you can more easily be happy for others. But it takes a lot of practiced attention to break out of those habits that we formed out of all of that subliminal messaging that we've been subjected to since we were little girls. As I notice and start to change those habits, I become more secure in my own worth and it becomes easier for me to support others.

In the business world, I kept trying to create systems that were more effective but I would get shot down because that's "just not how it's done." I was shocked to find that the "good old boys club" is still the norm, despite all the work of the women in the generations before me. I had created a business that had flexible hours and I could do a lot of work from home on my computer and make my own appointments. But it is hard to always work alone and the pay is unpredictable, so I was intrigued and hopeful when I was recruited to work on a team project. But after I paid a babysitter and filled my gas tank and drove to the meetings where I shared all of my brilliant ideas and did a large portion of the work, I found out that I was paid less than half the money that the men at the table were offered. I also learned that I made less than the young woman who couldn't figure out what project we were working on, but she sat next to the boss in her short skirt and touched his arm and looked at him with her gorgeous eyes and revealed cleavage that was not yet associated with feeding babies. My only consolation was that after I quit working on the project, all of the work came to a grinding halt and the project failed. But they typically can find another woman with children to feed and convince them to do all the work while the men take the credit.

"Unless a grain of wheat shall fall upon the ground and die, it shall remain but a single grain, and not give life." (9) We usually think of grain when it is ground up to make flour like when the Little Red Hen is looking for someone to help her make some bread. (10) Thinking of The Little Red Hen is actually a perfect story for tuning in to the second energy center. When we feel like we are not receiving the support and help that we need (probably from a block in the first energy center), we can feel like when we have something that we want to create, that we need to do it all ourselves. At each phase, from planting the seed, to reaping, to milling, to making the dough and baking the bread, she asks her neighbors and friends for help. We understand how she feels when she asks and they each say "not I." We know what it feels like when nobody hears us, and nobody cares about us. Some of us learn to just keep going, and do it all ourselves. She keeps going and she bakes the bread. And then they all show up to share in the reward and eat the bread. She did not receive the support and the love that she actually craved, but there is some triumph in the moment when she stands in her power and says that she will eat it all herself. (10)

Bread is the stuff of life. We ask for our daily bread as a way of receiving everything that we need to sustain our physical bodies. We break bread and share potluck dinners together as a sign of a caring community. We teach our kids to share and to be kind. But every good farmer knows that you need to set aside the best grain to be planted next spring to ensure next year's harvest.

That seed needs to be sacrificed and put back into the earth to die so that it can be transformed into more than just a seed. It needs to be nurtured with warmth and light from the sun and nutrients from good soil and water so that it can give life. As it lies beneath the soil it appears as if nothing is happening as you wait. Then, almost overnight, it seems to magically burst out of the soil and unfurls its green cotyledons (embryonic seed-leaves) to the sun. There is nothing like the magic of life sprouting forth from a seed to make you believe in miracles.

In the spring there are so many new things growing and changing every day that it is hard to even look at all of it. And this is why the signs of spring are often used as symbols of God's love for us. Like the giant oak tree that grows out of a tiny acorn, we have so much potential inside of us. Sometimes it is hard for us to see our own worth. We wrap too much of ourselves into our current reality and we fight against change. We think that our labels determine our identity. That acorn thinks it is small and insignificant and does not know that it is a mighty oak in concentrated form. When we start to feel our shell cracking and we feel our lives breaking apart at the seams, we do not stop and think about how miraculous it is that we no longer fit in that old shell. We panic and grasp at the pieces and hold on for dear life. I remember being a new mom and, despite wanting so badly to become a mother and then trying so hard and waiting for it, when it was finally here I

would have some days when I missed be
self. But my entire identity had changed an
no going back.

When I looked at the big picture of culture and
family and personal history, it was hard to figure out
what percentage of my symptoms were from my body
being worn out physically from the pregnancies or
from my society not valuing my contributions. Either
way, I started to be in pain again every day and my
asthma was back. I had joint pain (especially in my hips
and knees) and pelvic and abdominal pain worse than
ever. Again, I was having a really hard time getting a
diagnosis from a medical professional. The midwife
told me to go off of dairy so my hormones could
regulate. I was tested for arthritis because of my family
history of autoimmune diseases. The test results were
all negative, and then the doctor asked me if I could eat
more dairy!

Next, I went to a naturopath and she gave me a
regimen of homeopathic medicines and nutritional
supplements to first help me to detoxify my liver and
kidneys, and then build up good underlying health. I
felt like she was helping but I wanted to connect the
dots between how I carried those stories in my body
and the manifestation of the emotional blocks as

physical symptoms. I thought that I could connect with this naturopath who was also a mom and I shared my survivor story with her. It was still difficult for me to open up, but I was hoping that if I just got right to the point it would save us both some time. I was hoping that she would understand and be able to help, but she asked me why I was around boys in my childhood. It was such a bizarre question that I was stunned and felt rejected and shamed and I left without scheduling another appointment. I kept waiting for her to call me and follow up. She never did.

My inflammation improved from the naturopathic treatments though, and my menstrual cycles were a little less painful but it wasn't enough. In addition to those doctors I had also been seeing my chiropractor once or twice a week because I could not hold my spine in alignment. My abdominal muscles had completely separated from the twin pregnancy and although a diastasis is common in pregnancy, often just the top layer of muscles separate to make more room and then it knits back together afterwards. Some women find wearing an abdominal brace or belly binding to be helpful in the postpartum period as they heal. I loved how the brace helped my back feel a little better, but it made me sweat and I felt gross and stuck. I didn't know what else to try though because all three layers of my muscles had separated and I could put my entire hand into my belly between the left and right side of my abdominals. If a toddler jumped up on my lap their knees would go right into my guts because my organs were unprotected. I had to plan ahead and be really strategic about things like grocery shopping so that I would have help at the store and then help to bring the bags in from the minivan when I got home. I wished that I could lift my own kids onto the swings at the playground. They kept running faster and I couldn't keep up.

After my first birth I asked a trainer who had her degree in exercise science, to teach me how to regain my core strength. It hurt to walk, since those abdominal muscles wrap around and connect to your spine and are supposed to hold everything in place. I asked what exercises I could do to strengthen those core muscles again and I was sure to tell her that I had just had a cesarean. I didn't know how bad the diastasis was because none of the doctors had checked at my postpartum visit and nobody explained to me what it was. The crunches and Pilate's exercises that she showed me how to do actually made the separation get wider. I had really strong muscles on either side, but there was nothing in the middle. When I ate anything like salad that required some effort to digest my belly would keep hurting for about an hour after the meal. I liked to eat soup and yogurt.

I was really committed to natural and alternative health at this point and I had lost faith in the medical model, but my chiropractor and my physical therapist and my family doctor all told me that my diastasis required a surgical repair. They said that it would never knit back together on its own because the separation between the muscles was too wide. I had a CAT-SCAN that confirmed that it needed to be repaired surgically. I was already upset at having received this news and I couldn't even think about how to make that work while chasing toddlers and nursing a baby.

Then I found out that the insurance wouldn't cover it. They think that walking and eating and lifting your own kids is cosmetic and optional. They have only one code for diastasis repair and they don't make a distinction between whether it is a small cosmetic bulge and your belly does not lay as flat as it did before kids, or that your muscles have completely separated. I just wanted to live my life without being in pain and without seeing doctors every week. I wanted to go grocery shopping all by myself again. Was that too much to ask? It seems like these outdated beliefs that a woman is worth less than a man to society should be on their way out by now, especially considering how most of the medical professionals that I had seen were women.

I spent a long time trying to get the insurance company to support what all my doctors said was medically necessary. They actually told me that it was caused by pregnancy and that was my choice. I pointed out that the men who get a hernia from choosing to lift something that is too heavy have that repaired and those surgeries are covered. My kids are totally worth any sacrifice of course, but it would also be nice if I felt like my society valued my contribution of bringing these amazing people into the world to do incredible things. In the end, having to choose to pay for the surgery out of pocket became a test of how much I was worth to my family and how much I could accept my own self-worth.

I had just started getting better about paying for services as needed instead of being in pain. I would pay for Physical Therapy or Myofascial release and feel better in an hour instead of staying in pain. It was better for my family if I was not in bed all day. There was another practitioner that was covered by insurance, but by the time I went to multiple appointments spread over four weeks, it would end up costing almost the same amount anyway. So I learned to just say "yes" to what I needed and stop clinging to what no longer served me. I knew that the job that I did for my family was essential. And I would calculate out the cost of hiring multiple people to cover for all of the things that I did. And even if I could hire them all to drive and do laundry and clean and organize and care for the children and take care of my clients I would still have to coordinate all that and make sure that it all got done. It was more economical to pay all the money that I had earned that year on the surgery and then move on with my life without being in pain every day. I had been saving to buy something nice for my family, maybe renovate the house or take the kids on vacation. I chose to buy the kids a healthy mom instead.

This also meant that I stopped fighting the insurance company and decided that I'd move forward with a positive attitude and I'd earn the money doing something good instead of wasting more time and energy fighting for it. But as soon as I made the decision and chose the surgical team, I started to worry. I had dreams of dying in surgery and leaving my kids without a mother. With my life insurance I guess they could finally afford to pay a nanny, but I really couldn't imagine missing their childhood. I knew that no one could ever love them as much as I did. I knew how many millions of little details I was keeping in my head at all times. Even when my husband tried to cover my morning routine and make lunches and get them to the bus one day, I wrote out this really elaborate schedule with a crazy amount of detail on how each sandwich is different and which kid likes it cut in squares and which kid needs it cut diagonally. But I recorded the songs that I sing at bedtime just in case I wasn't there to tuck them in. Despite what society says, I knew that not only was my replacement cost too high; I was irreplaceable.

I started watching these videos online of another twin mom who had undergone the surgery that I needed. She recorded her experiences and shared the details so that other women could feel more prepared. She helped me to visualize and mentally prepare for all the details. After my cesarean they sent me home with zero instructions on wound care or scar therapy or how to recover from surgery while caring for two newborns. Nobody came to check on me. Nobody called to see if I was alive. I wish I could remember who the woman was in those videos because I'd love to thank her for her service. But this service should be the norm and not the exception. This kind of information should be provided by the medical professionals and not just shared by a mom who wanted to help other women like her. On her page there were women chatting in the comments section and it seemed like the insurance companies were not covering these surgeries anywhere in the country. For less money, you could fly to another country to have your surgery and then stay in a medical-spa while you recovered for two weeks. But I wanted to get home to my babies, so I opted for 24-hour American post-op "care" instead.

I was already unhappy about the treatment of mothers in this country, but then when I went to visit a friend in the hospital it really put the icing on the cake, so to speak. This friend is a man, and he had just had abdominal surgery. When I went to visit, the nurses came in to see how he was doing and they were so gentle and kind and asked if they could get him anything to make him more comfortable. Nobody made fun of him for being in pain or told him to get out of bed and go take care of other people. There was not a hint of coercion or sarcasm, just good-old fashioned compassion. So, I guess there is post-op care in this country, just not for mothers.

I remember getting the bill from the surgeon, and then one for the anesthesiologist, and one for the hospital, too. This was my last chance to change my mind. They had to be paid up front, before they would operate. I remember exactly where I was when I was driving in my car and asking God what I should do. I had been feeling like I had to do this alone. I felt like God was so far away and I couldn't feel His presence like I usually do. I didn't like that feeling and I had been so scared for weeks. I can still picture exactly which exit ramp I was driving past when the image of footprints on a beach popped into my mind. The punch line of the "Footprints in the Sand" poem followed quickly. (12) I hadn't been alone after all. God was not far away. I had been feeling so out of control because I was being carried and I am used to being in charge of handling everything. Once again, I would need to learn how to let go. I needed to trust and I needed to have faith.

We scheduled the surgery for the beginning of summer since my husband teaches and would be home for the summer. . He could take care of the house and the kids while I recovered. I figured this was as good a time as any because the baby was still small and soon I'd have all of them running faster than me. There was no reason to put it off and be in pain for another year. I asked my mother to come and help since she's a nurse, and unlike when we were waiting for the twins to be born, she was retired from her job at the doctor's office now. I explained that I understood that she doesn't like to cook or clean, but she could hold the baby and read books and do puzzles with the kids so that my husband could mow the lawn and get dinner on the table. I am still shaking my head about this one, but she said that she couldn't come and stay with us and help me with my recovery because my husband might watch baseball. I'm still not sure why it is so bad if he watches the game at the end of a long day after he's done all the work of caring for everyone. He usually just listens to it on the radio while he mows the lawn or washes the dishes anyway. But I think one time when she came to visit he used the game as an excuse to go hide because he was getting stressed out about having company. So she pictured having to do all the work while he went and relaxed. Even if I had that kind of husband, wouldn't that be even more reason for my mom to come help me with my recovery?

Anyway, at the time I still just couldn't believe that she wasn't coming. I cried to my midwife about it and she offered to drive me to the hospital for my surgery. Since she wasn't family, they wouldn't let her past the check-in station, which meant that I had to go through the hardest part completely alone. I have always had body issues, even long before I had the "twin-skin" on my belly, so the pre-op was even worse than the surgery. I had to stand there behind a flimsy curtain completely naked and have them take pictures and draw on me with markers while they talked about me like I was a slab of meat. I guess paying cash doesn't get you any star treatment. Then when it is time for your surgery, you really have to give away all of your control and just trust and have faith when they put you under general anesthesia. I laid on that table completely alone and hoped that I would wake up to see my family again.

When I woke up in the hospital bed, I met my roommate and her whole family. They couldn't believe that my family wasn't coming. She had enough visitors to spare though, so someone came and sat by my bed and asked about my kids and kept me company. When the nurse came, I asked her a question about what I was feeling, but she didn't even seem to know what surgery I'd had. I was asking about my sutures because they were really uncomfortable where there was a big knot through the layers of muscle just under the center of my ribcage. It felt like the sutures were pulling in a weird way and I wanted to make sure that it was okay.

The nurse just pointed to the bikini line incision which was where the surgeon had cut through my skin to gain access to my insides so that he could suture the layers of abdominal muscles together. I was asking about my diastasis repair and I just wanted to be reassured that everything was going to be fine. She was pointing at the stitches that she could see on the surface and acting like I was wrong about the location of my pain. She wasn't listening, and she wouldn't even come closer to the bed so that she could feel what I was talking about. She dismissed my pain and didn't acknowledge my worry. I was already feeling abandoned and unloved by my family, and then I felt like I couldn't even pay a health care professional to take care of me physically.

I tried to sleep. I thought it would be relaxing to have a night without any kids in my bed. But when I tried to move a pillow and get somewhat comfortable, I realized that my breasts were rock-hard and hugely engorged because the baby was not there to nurse. I hadn't even felt them get full, and I kind of forgot I even had breasts because they were so numb from the morphine. I had packed a hand-operated breast pump and I tried to use it, but the milk just poured all over me because I couldn't sit up to hold the bottle upright. The nurse seemed annoyed with me because I had pushed the call button and asked her to come and help me change my gown and get some towels. I finally went to sleep, and then I jerked awake with a huge pain. I had pulled on all of the newly placed sutures when I had jumped in my nightmare. After the painful startling from the second or third terrifying nightmare, I told the nurse that the medication didn't seem to agree with me. I asked about other options that might have less painful side-effects. I was in a hospital but I couldn't get them to write me a prescription for something else for my pain. I had to call my family doctor on her cell phone. She called in a prescription to my local pharmacy and my husband brought the new medicine to me in the morning. It was a long night.

Aside from actually making the choice that I deserved to heal, another good thing that came out of the surgery was seeing how many friends had offered to help. One family watched the kids while my husband came to get me in the morning and drove me home on the most painful ride in a car, ever. Another friend was a postpartum doula and she knew how to set up a website with volunteer time-slots so that my friends could take turns dropping off dinner or helping with the kids. One of the doulas from my networking group came over and bounced my baby on her knee and sang to him and she read a story to my kids. I was glad for the kids to get some much needed attention, but it broke my heart at the same time that I couldn't hold my own baby. I was so grateful for my friends, but sad at the same time. It seems to be one of the universal truths of motherhood that you will rarely ever get to have just one emotion at a time.

Even with the help of our friends, my husband was once again the primary caregiver. I felt like we had had enough of the poorer and the sicker half of our wedding vows and I longed for the day when we could try the richer and healthier half. When we were first together I would get up from the bed and go brush my hair so that he wouldn't see my bed-head in the morning. Even after living together for all those years, sharing a bed, and birthing our children, I still wanted to impress him and wanted him to think that I was beautiful. But when nobody else was there to help, I had to let him help me to the bathroom and he had to change the dressings over my incision. He also helped me empty my drains, which was so much more disgusting than either of us could have imagined.

I was glad that the woman on the videos had warned me, because the doctor and nurses didn't really tell me much about that, and even when they did, they mentioned it like it was no big deal. Emptying the big plastic bags that were now strapped to my body to collect the bloody goo that was draining out of my belly was super gross, and I have to say, not the most romantic part of our relationship. I thought I would be happy to see them go, but as soon as it was time to pull the drains out, I wished that I had just left them in. Again, I'm not sure how my totally non-medically-trained husband became the one for the job, but anyway, here we were on our own at home left to figure this out ourselves. He started pulling on the drains as instructed, but I had no idea how long they were. They just kept coming. I had thought they were little ports just inside my skin that let the extra fluid drain out, but as he started pulling it became obvious that they went all the way up from my pubic area to my ribs and had started to kind of adhere to the underside of my skin. Having those huge plastic things inside of me might have contributed to those pains that I was trying to ask the nurse at the hospital about and a little explanation would have been helpful.

So anyway, let's skip ahead to the happy part of the story when one day, a few months later, I was driving in my minivan and I realized that when singing along with the radio, I could actually sing out in my full voice again. I had strong abdominal muscles and I could project my voice. I had totally forgotten about singing when I made my pros/cons list. There are a lot of things that we use our abs for that we take entirely for granted. After the surgery, it was ten weeks before I could stand up straight and it took years for us to catch up on the gardening and housekeeping projects that got neglected that summer, but in the end it was so worth it. I was worth it. The next summer when it was hot and sweaty and I was able to walk without having to wear a tight, sweaty abdominal brace, I knew that it was really paying off. And when I danced with my husband at the Christmas party again, it was priceless.

The time that I spent sitting on the couch and healing also created the opportunity for reflection and for writing. I finished writing my first book while I recovered from that surgery, during nap time while the older kids were in school. As I wrote my birth story, I thought a lot about Magdalena. I had a lovely friend with that name in graduate school, and when we picked out two boy names and two girl names for my first pregnancy that name was on the list. But as time went on, I explored more and more about the historic woman who has become legend. While thinking of how we hold these wounds around our worth and value in our second chakra, I thought a lot about Mary Magdalene and how her reputation was ruined by one nasty rumor. She was originally known as the one who was closest to Jesus, the apostle who stayed by his side at the foot of the cross and was the first to witness the risen Lord at Easter. Her anointing Him with precious oil was what made Jesus become known as *The Anointed*, otherwise translated as *the Christ*. And then 500 years later one man called her a prostitute in his homily, even though they never used that word in the bible, and then the rumor spread through the centuries and around the globe. In 1969 they printed a retraction saying that it was never true, but quite a few years later, many people still have trouble shifting their understanding of her story. (13)

Historically, women are either portrayed as pure or wicked. Women can never seem to just have the freedom to be real. They use stories about Jesus' mother Mary and Mary Magdalene (who were the two powerful women who were central in Jesus' life, and who helped to start the church) to perpetuate the virgin/whore dichotomy. For me, the Magdalene came to represent someone who was misunderstood by history. It reminded me of how I always try to be a nice person and to help others, but my intentions are often misunderstood. I am always trying so hard and feel like I have to perfect and I feel like I'll never be enough. I am so critical of myself, but I can see the good in everyone else. So it hurts when people feel like I am judging them, when really I am trying to be of service. In other ways too, the way that I am received is not usually in line with how I feel inside, and I have spent most of my life trying to figure out why people can't see the real me. As a woman, I have tried to live up to this ideal of being pure and I have always felt guilty and ashamed because I have never found it to be possible. Just like mine, I am sure that Mary's story is complex and complicated and real. Maybe because I have walked through this world feeling misunderstood, I have connected with the Magdalene's story in such a personal way. Despite the pervasive rumors, I can sense the truth of who Mary was, standing strong against the public scorn and turning the other cheek throughout the generations, just like Jesus taught us.

The Magdalene is also associated with sensuality, which terrifies most men because they think it is the same as sexuality. Maybe that makes men fearful because they feel they can be led astray by their sexual attractions and urges. Sensuality really means to be able to connect to your divinity through your senses. In this modern culture where we rely on technology and put our faith in machines, we are cut off from nature. We are so out of touch with our own feelings and maybe just sensing things with our bodies at all sounds scary. But if we learn to tune in to what we feel (physically and emotionally) and learn to be present in this moment, and we reconnect with nature and go within and reconnect with our own truth, then we can reclaim our power and truly be healthy. After all, maybe that power is what made the Magdalene so intimidating.

When we learn to tune in to what our bodies are telling us, we can feel when we have something that isn't working correctly. I think it is odd when healthy people rely on technological gadgets to monitor their heart rate. If your heart is racing and you are breathing heavily because you just ran a mile, than you know it is totally normal. If you are sitting still and it starts doing that, then you should notice and investigate possible causes. I am not judging anyone who uses personal health equipment as a way to help them reconnect with their bodies with the intention of improving their physical health. I do wonder though if this is just another way that we are giving control to external forces instead of learning to have in internal locus of control. I think a large part of taking our power back can be in learning to listen to our bodies and honor and respect the information that we are given. We can learn to feel when we have a healthy flow of energy through our systems and then see the patterns and look for the root causes when something feels off.

When I think of how we get these blocks that keep our energy from flowing, it always reminds me of our old oak tree. At the beginning of this chapter I talked about recognizing the miracle in that there is all the potential of a tree inside of the tiny acorn. At this point in my journey though, I was reflecting on the other end of life when the tree is old and it starts to wither and fade. One spring I noticed that the old tree had one large section that did not burst into color with a million baby leaves. Then another large branch was leafless. Soon the whole tree was bare. I thought that maybe it would be blown down in a storm, but oak is a hardwood and that dead tree stood its ground against the strongest winds.

I finally called a tree expert to come and take the old tree down. When he came to remove the tree I asked him to let me know if he could tell why it had died. He mentioned that sometimes a large root gets cut by a road-crew when they resurface the road, or snipped by a snowplow in the winter. He said a sudden trauma of that size to a single root can shock the whole system and the tree never recovers. But as he cut the tree down one piece at a time, starting at the top and working his way down, all of a sudden his saw hit a metal chain in the trunk of the tree. I had never seen it because it was overgrown long before I found this property and became the steward of these trees. With all of the layers of bark, the chain had stayed there unseen, but it had been cutting off the flow of life force through the tree. When I think of an emotional block that is keeping us from letting our life force flow through our bodies, I picture that chain. In my own life, I try to look past the layers of armor that I have grown to protect myself, so that I can find the chains and release them before they are so grown in that I can't even see them, but I know that the effects of those old traumas are still there because I can feel how they are blocking me from living fully.

Things to think about:

- What chains are blocking you from living up to your full potential? What is it that you were meant to create or to bring into this world? What is keeping you from creating?

- Are there any relationships where you do not feel valued? Where do you feel that you give pieces of yourself away?

- Do you feel like you are enough? Do you measure yourself by all the things that you do, or can you see your own worth regardless of what you can give? Do you feel replaceable?

- How can you choose YOU today?

- Where do you need to crack yourself open to make room for growth and change? Visualize the new shell that better fits the new YOU. Remember, it is okay to grow in stages.

Chapter 3: Shaping Our Identity

It was good to finally understand that so many of my physical symptoms were rooted in how I was carrying those unresolved, emotional wounds (for myself and for those in my family who had never been able to heal) in those first two, foundational energy centers. I think that keeping those secrets and holding all of that shame in my root blocked the flow to my third chakra and that is why I had so much trouble feeling my own power or owning my identity. I somehow always knew that I had so much potential, and there were parts of me that were smart and accomplished, but then at the same time I felt like I was always plagued by doubt and low self-esteem. I like things to make sense, so this discrepancy between how I felt and who I knew that I truly could be bothered me.

When the third chakra is blocked, we feel it in our gut. When someone attacks you personally, they say it feels like a punch in the gut. If your life is full of chronic stress, you actually gain weight around the waist to protect yourself. If you don't have the stomach for it, you could develop ulcers or heartburn. When you don't learn to tune in to your gut instincts, or when you ignore what your gut is telling you, some may say that you didn't follow through because you don't have the guts.

I find it interesting that even people who say that they don't believe in energy centers will still call you "yellow-bellied" or "lily-livered," referring to the yellow of the third energy center, because it shows that the ancient knowledge about the chakras is built into our cultural language. Each chakra is associated with a color that you can use to tune in to that vibration during meditation, starting at the base chakra with red, and following the colors of the rainbow from the lower frequency to the highest at the crown chakra. The higher frequency colors like blue and indigo are vibrating faster. You can also tune in to this with musical notes, making a lower sound as you tune in to your root, and then higher sounds at each level. Start with Do at the base and continue with Ray, Me, Fa, So, La and Ti at the crown. I like that "Me" occurs at the third chakra when you focus on issues to do with your identity and personal power. When they say to "raise your vibration," it is referring to bringing your attention from focusing on survival (money, sex and power) and up into higher thinking (love, beauty, gratitude, and joy) and to focusing more on the spiritual than on the physical. (*See appendix*)

We develop our self-identity during the third year of our life, and those behaviors of defining and declaring what we like and what we don't like are often why that year after our second birthday is referred to as "the terrible twos." Sometimes two-year-olds may not have any way to know if they like something yet, but they say "no" just to see what reaction they get from their defiance. Sometimes they just refuse to go along with your idea to get in some practice at asserting their independence. This is the phase of mothering where we learn to choose our battles. If we let them refuse to eat that particular food now, they'll probably end up liking it just fine later. If we let them wear something that is totally inappropriate for the weather or is outlandish or doesn't match, we can secretly pack other outfits or bring a jacket even if they insist that it is not cold outside, and then we're not arguing with them, but we're prepared for when they change their mind later. If we allow them to explore their own identity and who they are as individuals, not just as a part of the family and not just as an attachment of their mother, then there will be the opportunity for health in the third energy center.

I tried my best to let my children develop positive self-esteem at two years old by letting them each decide who they would be that day. I kept a cedar chest full of costumes and a bin of extra fabric in a variety of colors handy and I'd quickly throw together costumes for whoever it was that they insisted that they were that day whether it was pirates or princesses, knights or dinosaurs or butterflies. Giving them that strong foundation and letting them grow their roots and then spread their wings will ideally allow them to develop a healthy sense of self. They will be able to trust their gut. They will be able to make decisions with confidence and not be intimidated. Hopefully my children will know that they can come and tell me anything about who they are and what they are thinking about.

As a parent, the terrible twos can be a tough phase,

because while I want my children to feel free to be themselves, I also want them to be socially aware that others have needs too. I don't want them to be selfish, but I also don't want them to think that their needs are less important than anyone else's. While they test their boundaries, as their parents we can help them to find that delicate balance. They are learning to be aware of their surroundings while learning to see themselves as separate and unique. At this age, we start to take them out to more play dates so that they can be social butterflies and learn to interact with other children, and so that they can learn to share and to take turns. I see adults every day that did not spend enough time learning this skill when they were children. Some people take too much and only think of themselves, and others don't give themselves enough credit and they give too much of themselves away. The better we get at walking that balance beam ourselves, the better we will be at modeling that for our kids.

Another thing that I've learned about developing the seven energy centers as we grow is that we spiral through them again every seven years. So, if children don't get a good dose of asserting themselves as toddlers and they feel like they are being oppressed, a focus on defining their self-identity comes around again when they are 9 and then 16 years old. Just when you think you've survived one phase of parenting you find that it just rolls into another.

I learned something about this when I thought that I was done with the teething phase, but I was mistaken. I've since learned that it is never done. I had a really miserable, grumpy kid one day and didn't realize that they were teething since I had thought of that as a toddler-phase. When they are little and they are fussy everyone says "oh, they must be teething." But just when you think they are done and you've survived that phase, then their molars come in. But at that age they've started school and they are supposed to know how to behave. Then they start losing their baby teeth and growing bigger teeth. They look at their classmate's toothless grin and wonder when they will lose their first tooth. They anticipate the moment and they get excited when they reach that rite of passage. But the growing pains are there, too. After a while, they get used to it and they just pull the tooth out by themselves and forget to even tell you about it. Then they grow more molars. If you have multiple ages of children in your house it may seem like someone is always teething.

Maybe if we teach the children to stay tuned in to

what their bodies are telling them, as they get older they can come to us and say that their teeth hurt instead of just being grumpy and making us guess as to what is going on. It reminds me of when they were babies and we had to try to figure out what was upsetting them while we just wanted to cry too. I kept thinking that maybe it would get easier when they learned to talk, but even then I often feel like I still need to ask twenty questions to get to the real reason why they are upset. How funny is it that when you are trying so hard to get the answer out of them they say that it is like pulling teeth? To teach the children this skill of listening to their bodies, it would be good if the grown-ups had developed it themselves. Even adults who are experiencing dental pain don't open by telling people that they are in pain. They head in to work thinking they can pretend that they feel fine, but then they bite their coworkers head off over something trivial. We often just keep going because there are so many things that need to get done, but we might start to lose patience a little more quickly than when we are feeling good. When we are in pain, we have a lowered tolerance for everything else, and we all act a little bit like toddlers having a tantrum. One of the good things about spiraling through each of these phases, is that if we missed developing these skills in our own childhood, we can learn them alongside our children this time through.

◆

I know that I have some blocks in my third chakra, because my self-image is so skewed, but when I tried to discover what I needed to heal, it was hard to think of what could have happened to me during those early years. I don't remember as much about when I was 2 years old, but when I was 9, I remember having a really awful birthday party, and I remember that I refused to eat oranges. I told my Brownie Leader that I was allergic to oranges and that I needed a different snack. I think it was just that we ate orange slices after every soccer game and I was simply getting tired of them. I know that with a new baby brother in my house that I must have been craving some extra attention, and I liked how nice my leader was about stuff like that. I eat oranges now and I love them, but I'm wondering if there is some connection to this 3rd chakra because then I really developed a serious food allergy when I was 16 years old.

Having a food allergy can really start to define you, especially when you have to be careful to check the ingredients or ask about everything that you eat. Food is so central to our cultural identity and to our relationships. We share a special meal with our family for the holidays. We gather with friends to eat food and celebrate everything from birthdays to football games. When we start dating it is traditional to get asked out to dinner. So this symptom became a central part of my identity. When a healer first asked me how old I was when I developed my food allergy, I got goosebumps because I immediately realized that I had my first anaphylactic reaction (which my family noticed) the same year that I had lost my baby (which they didn't notice.)

I can only guess, but I think that it may have been easier to navigate my teens if I had more confidence in myself. The problem with trying to develop self-esteem at 16 years old (when I spiraled through another big third chakra growth year) is that by then I was looking at myself through the eyes of the boys. When they would say that I was too ugly for them to date me, I internalized that belief. I knew that it was true because even my own best friend and my family called me ugly. Those words hurt me so deeply that they left me vulnerable to a man who said the sweetest things, even while he was hurting me. When I was raped I knew that I would never be able to be the good girl that I wanted to be, and I didn't know who I was supposed to be anymore. I lost all grip on what was real. I stopped eating. I stopped sleeping. Some days I thought about killing myself. Mostly I just went through the motions of the life that I had planned before I had lost what was left of my innocence and of my identity. When I think of that young girl now, I try to send her messages that she is loved. I tell her to hang in there. In some way, maybe it worked because even when I was in the midst of those dark years, I somehow knew that someday it would be okay, and that I would use what I learned from my pain to help others. Maybe what kept pushing me forward through those struggles was actually my future self, reaching across the years and whispering in my ear that it was going to get better and that it was worth staying to see how it all played out.

Sixteen is the age when we jump off the bridge just because all of our friends are doing it. I asserted my independence by leaving the house in the middle of the night or walking down the railroad tracks. Many of my friends were even more disillusioned and depressed than I was and we didn't know where to turn for help. We grieved together as we lost multiple friends to suicide. I didn't know how to go back to school and sit next to my classmates who had stood and cheered while my friend was murdered for being different. Somehow I survived high school. I am still here. I just kept putting one foot in front of the other. I had to keep trusting that the trail would lead me to the other side of the mountain.

Now I'm the mother and I try not to let my fear take over, but as my children move through each stage, I'm preparing for the challenging teenage years ahead. I know that I probably won't ever have the right answer, but I'm hoping that my efforts to instill confidence in them when they are small will give them a little bit of a buffer as they grow and head out into the world. I want them to know that they can always turn to me in times of trouble. I don't want them to stuff their pain inside and let it make them sick.

When we develop blocks in this third energy center, the act of choosing what we think we are supposed to instead of choosing what we really want, or the stress over each decision can lead to ulcers and indigestion. Chronic stress is marked by carrying extra weight around your waist to protect your third energy center. Our fear and our inability to trust our gut causes problems with digestion and we develop symptoms in our intestines or our colon. Resentment can really become a big pain in the butt. When you feel like you have no power to make choices for your own life it can manifest as Irritable Bowel Syndrome or Crohn's Disease. Letting these patterns go on for decades can lead to cancers in these areas as well. (14) I had so many of those physical symptoms starting when I was 16 years old, even though they never fit with a single diagnosis. I wanted to heal them though, and not let them grow into something even more serious like they had for so many of my relatives. I needed to learn to follow my gut. I needed to find my courage. The color that you can meditate on to strengthen your 3rd chakra is yellow. Personally, when I feel like life gives me a gut-punch or I just don't have the stomach for it, I like to picture a big yellow sunflower, standing tall and strong, and blooming with its face turned towards the sunshine.

When my giant oak came down in the front yard there was already another tree growing in that vacated spot, reaching for the newly available patch of sun, with plenty of space to stretch out its growing limbs. Sometimes people transplant a tree but they don't dig a large enough hole to soften the earth around it and it doesn't have enough room to stretch out its roots. Instead of stretching out and widening the tree's base of support, the roots spiral around in the tight hole and choke each other. We need to give our children roots, but then also carve out opportunities for them to stretch out and explore and reach out to the community and receive an even greater base of support. When we ourselves have issues with courage and self-esteem, it can be really hard to know how to give that to our kids.

My grandmother gave me these beautiful irises from her yard and I planted them where they would get plenty of sun. I knew that the iris plants spread from the root and make new babies each year and continue to spread and that they need to be divided and given more room. So I planted them next to this giant fossil rock figuring that they'd fill in the garden bed and then when they reached the rock they would turn and grow roots in the other direction. Little did I know that those delicate looking flowers could in fact move a huge rock. I often think of those flowers. They remind me of how something tiny can drive a wedge in something that you thought was solid. They remind me of how little I know about so many things. But they are also a symbol of how you can move mountains, even if someone else underestimates you.

Once upon a time my mother-in-law told me that I was "no shrinking violet." I am putting that on my list of things that people did not intend as a compliment but I will take it as high praise anyway. When I was reading up on baby names, I read that one of the saints named after Mary Magdalene was "no shrinking violet," so

I figured the name was a perfect fit for a daughter of mine. I would actually love to be a people-pleaser. I would love to go with the crowd and be popular and have friends and be included. But I guess it is my lot to always have to push that edge. As a teacher, I work right at the edge of their comfort zone and then challenge them to look over the edge. I bring their awareness to something that needs to be acknowledged so they can begin to change. Although it is actually my instinct to shrink and play small to feel safe, I know that if I don't stand my ground then it will just come around again on the next spiral or fall to someone else to do the work. So in those moments when I feel like I am looking over the edge, I try to say "yes" to the opportunities (that often present themselves as challenges) that are put in my path. I try to just follow instructions when I am led by the spirit. And sometimes, when I meet with what seem like impossible obstacles, instead of turning around, I just keep growing slowly and gathering resources until what seemed like a huge obstacle starts to move. These are what I call "*Magdalena Moments.*"

As moms, we try to give our kids the world. We want all of these amazing things for them and we try to create opportunities and we run ahead removing obstacles from their path. We want them to be happy and healthy. We try to keep them safe. It would be hard to keep putting one foot in front of the other if we admitted to ourselves how powerless we feel at times. Each kid comes with their own story. They have their own soul purpose and things that they came here to accomplish. It might not be as obvious as the kid that practically dances out of the womb or the one that nurses all of their stuffed animals back to health, but their particular path will be revealed more and more over time. We try our best to help our children to discover and use their gifts and to develop their natural talents into useful skills. Sometimes it is harder to accept their limitations. Letting go of our own expectations for their life is hard. Letting go of our hopes and dreams is harder.

There are so many collective beliefs that we cling to even when all of the evidence to the contrary is right there in front of us. Maybe we tell ourselves some of these stories so that we can keep going. We imagine that every baby will be born perfectly healthy and then live in a world where nothing bad ever happens and they grow up to be beautiful, smart and accomplished adults who live happily ever after. Of course all of our children will live long enough to be grandparents themselves and then die peacefully in their sleep surrounded by people who love and respect them. That is the universal dream that so many of us cling to and then we act shocked when reality breaks through and wakes us from that dream. They say that parents should not outlive their children. But it happens every day. So many women that I know have lost a child. There are so many invisible mothers who are grieving alone without the support of their communities. I wonder if when we say things like that it shouldn't be like this, we are just adding to this feeling that their life ended when they lost their child. What if that happened when they had many more years on their journey? It happens all the time. That feeling that things are not as they should be and that you are not as you should be can become a part of your identity.

Whenever there is sad news or horrible tragedy I hear people say "I can't believe it." Why is everybody always so shocked? I find that it just keeps us from taking action. We can only make choices in the present moment. We can only act on the information that we have at the time. At the same time though, I feel like we need some hope for a brighter future to get us through today. We change another diaper and stay up singing another song when we can barely keep our eyes open, all the while daydreaming about how proud we'll be at their graduation. We teach them to tie their shoes in hopes that they'll head off on grand adventures one day, but a part of us is scared to let them go. We braid their hair and picture how beautiful they will be on their wedding day. But things rarely go the way we plan them in our daydreams. So how do we walk that fine line between letting them go and holding them close and keeping them safe?

I awoke from a really vivid dream, suddenly sweating and out of breath. I wrote it down quickly in my journal before it faded away because I knew this one was important. In my dream, everyone was walking up to this deep, dark quarry and putting things in that they needed to let go. We are attached to so many worldly things and giving them too much importance weighs us down. It can make us too tired for the journey, or can cause us to sway from our path. We keep busy with maintaining our possessions and even our relationships for too long instead of letting go at the right time. In my dream, various people were coming up to the quarry and dropping in their most prized possessions. If they didn't let go when they heaved it over the edge, then they'd fall with it. I had to go and push my new car over the edge and watch it sink. I had just bought it with the money that I'd made from my own business and not from my husband's salary and it was a sign of my success. But I had to let it go. I didn't know that that was the easy part.

As I walked to the edge of the quarry to watch my new car sinking below the dark water, I saw a head of blond hair in the water. As soon as I saw it, I knew it was my son. I wasn't ready to let my little boy go. They couldn't ask that of me. I woke in a panic. Just that day he had fallen on the playground. He'd hit his throat on the bar and came running over to me clutching his neck. I thought that he couldn't breathe, and even after I realized that it was just sore, it had taken a while for my heart to start beating again. When I woke from this dream I went to check his bed. He was fine, but I stood by his bed and watched him breathe for a bit. Then I checked on my other children. And then I mourned the fact that I really have no control. I have no choice. There are no guarantees that I get to keep them. Some children come for only a few hours or a few days. How was I to know or who was I to say how long I would have my babies with me?

One of the women in my support group for cesarean moms was expecting her first little girl and preparing for her VBAC. I hadn't known how to let go of all of those little girl clothes when Magdalena never came, but this was the perfect opportunity and I happily gave her all of those little pink outfits. We were all so excited for her birth. None of us could imagine that her baby would not stay. I could barely keep functioning when I heard the news. And she wasn't even mine. I had experienced loss in my own way, but I had never had to bury one of my children. I had made it this long without ever having seen a tiny, beautiful baby in a casket. But how could I even think of grieving when my friend was the one who had to let her baby go?

It is all too big. No one knows how to make space for something that big. We shield our hearts because if we really allow ourselves to feel the immensity of it, we are afraid that we won't be able to keep going. So we cry in the shower and dry our tears and go make sandwiches and walk our kids to the bus stop. And we say about a million prayers each day. And then we breathe a huge sigh of relief when the big yellow school bus comes around the bend and brings them home safely, when the fever breaks, when the cast comes off, when we are blessed with another day together.

And who has time to think of these things at all when the kids are small? One challenging phase runs into another. You are so busy cleaning their artwork off of your newly painted wall that you sometimes forget to be impressed by their creativity. You might have been so flustered that you didn't even notice that when they wrote their name on the table in marker they didn't get any of the letters backwards this time. And you can't decide whether to be angry or impressed that they were smart enough to sign their brother's name and tried to get them in trouble instead.

Often our biggest blessings are also our largest responsibility. I've always been terrified to have anything nice because it would just be taken away. In Amy Tan's books she writes about how in Chinese culture you can't praise your children because then it will attract bad spirits and they will be taken away. (15) (I think maybe the Puritans have a similar belief and that's why they can't let anyone know that they love their children.) The more you look, the more you will find the intertwining of fear and love. We are proud of each new milestone and want to celebrate our child's new accomplishment, at the same time that we grieve the phase that they have left behind. As they walk away and shape their own identities, we are excited to get to know the person that they are becoming, but we also kind of wish that we could always hold them close and keep them safe.

When I was first married, every time my husband

got home later than I expected I'd picture him dead in a ditch and would try to imagine how I would live without him. I didn't want that future, so I willed him to come home safely. And then when he walked through the door I'd yell at him for making me feel like that. In my heart I was really relieved and wanted to cling to him and keep him close, but I pushed him away. I was afraid to need him so much and to love him so deeply. Then we had kids and he became even more a part of me. Now I'm the mother to four totally different children and I try to help them to become who they are meant to be, giving them room to grow, but I can't see what is ahead on their path. I wish that I could hold them close and keep them safe. I try not to push them away. I try not to let my fears overwhelm my love and come out as anger. But if I mess up and sound annoyed instead of relieved, I can always go back at another time and sit them down and explain to them how they scared me and why I was so emotional because I love them so much.

One day while the kids were in school and the baby was at daycare, I sat at the office trying to finish up some paperwork before the staff meeting when the weirdest feeling came over me. I was typing at the computer station when suddenly all of the energy drained out of my body, like someone had pulled the plug out of a bathtub drain. I didn't know what had come over me but I tried to finish my work. The only problem was that I couldn't read the words on the computer screen. It was like I knew that I should understand, but the symbols were just some secret code. The only other time I had felt like that was during labor when I went into transition and the logical part of my brain just shut off, but I wasn't even pregnant, and certainly not in labor. I tried to go to the meeting, walking across the room like I was in a trance, but I couldn't understand what they were saying. The woman at the front desk was worried about me driving, but somehow I got home. I guess I'd been driving long enough that it was muscle memory and instinct by that point.

As soon as I got home I fell down on my bed and went to sleep. The kids came home from school and I just laid there. I never really lay down in the middle of the day because I'm afraid if I stop moving I'll never get up again, so they didn't know what to do. I'm not sure how many times the phone rang before I finally heard it and answered. It was my sister calling to tell me about how my brother's wife had just drowned while they were on vacation at the beach. I fell back in my bed and when I slept it was like my sister-in-law took me through the whole thing in my dream and I understood how she felt when she died. I kind of knew then, but I had it explained better later by an energy healer, that I had automatically sent all of my energy to my brother to give him the strength to hold on to her a little longer until the boat came to rescue him and to bring her body to shore.

It took a while to bring her body home to her mother because they were overseas. I didn't get to talk to him much because he was busy taking care of international paperwork and details and he was also being treated for his own injuries. When we were finally able to have the wake at the funeral home in the town where she grew up, I could finally hug him. I simply held space for him as he had to go through it again and again as everyone who had just read about it in the newspaper came through the receiving line to say how shocked they were. They told him that they couldn't believe it. I remember so distinctly how he said that he believed it, because he had lived it. When there was a lull in the crowd and we had a moment, he explained to me how he had swam out into the ocean to find her after a huge wave had swept her up and over the rocks at the side of the natural pool where they send all the tourists to go relax. He climbed over the rocks and went over the coral reef and he found her body, but she was already gone.

He was running out of strength trying to hold onto her and he was getting pulled under by the current, but he didn't know if he could let her go. How do you choose when either option will take all of your courage and strength? Thank God the boat came to scoop them both up out of the sea at just that moment because having to choose is what leaves the heaviest weight on our souls.

I had found this health and healing store in my hometown where they sell all sorts of things-- whenever I had to choose a gift, I would go in there and buy things that were more meaningful than shopping at the department store. The women who owned the small shop were always so helpful, so I'd go in and say, "My friend just bought a new house. What do I get them?" and they'd give me something that was supposed to bring good energy into the new space. This time I went in with a heavy heart and I asked them to help me find something to bring to a man whose heart is broken and who needs to find the strength to go on. They brought me to these stones that help hold the pieces of your soul together while your heart is shattering into a million pieces. As soon as I looked in the bin, there was this one stone that drew my eye, and it had a dark pattern on the stone that looked like my sister-in-law had drawn it herself. I had just gotten a hand-painted vase from her for Christmas and it had cute stick figures of each member of our family, and each one was unique. She was always making homemade and thoughtful things like that. On this stone was a stick figure of a woman dancing in a triangle shaped dress. And it was the perfect size to fit between your thumb and fingers and to have as a worry stone in your pocket, so I gave it to my brother at the funeral home.

I also had the impossible job of having to figure out how to tell my children that their beloved aunt had died, and help them to understand but in a way that would not make them afraid to live their own lives. When I first told them that she had gone to heaven, we created our own ceremony for her at home and we wrote her notes and drew her pictures and then threw them on the campfire to be sent up to her in the smoke. We asked the angels to take good care of her. Each kid picked out pretty, glittery beads that reminded us of her and we strung the beads. We decided to give those to my brother as well so that he would have a tangible reminder of our love for her. It helped the kids to have something to do with their hands while they processed the news and grieved in their hearts. It was important to give them that time at home to sit with their own feelings before we had to pack the suitcases into the minivan and travel to visit with family.

Not knowing how long we would have to wait for her to be brought home so that we could have the wake and the funeral made it even more difficult for the children. It ended up being almost two weeks, so they went to school and we tried to keep going with our routine, but I called the teachers to let them know to be extra gentle with them if they weren't acting like themselves. We ended up having the calling hours on my twins' birthday. I swear we can never have just one emotion at a time. Luckily my husband has family that lives close to where the services were, so after we drove down and paid our respects, they were able to take the kids and celebrate their birthday while my husband and I went back to the funeral home to be there for my brother during another impossibly hard day.

My little brother was born when I was three years old and he was my first baby. I always felt so close to him even though we'd lived far apart since high school, but now we were standing side-by-side and I felt like I couldn't reach him at all. I didn't know how to help him. I felt like he was here in body, but part of his soul had gone with her. I had felt it when he had reached all the way across the ocean to call on me for strength, but it wasn't enough to save him from the heartache. I was crying for him, and for my own loss of an amazing friend and my new sister, and for my kids who had lost a beautiful aunt, but I was also grieving the loss of this idea that I could ever keep them safe.

Apparently life is unpredictable and you never know how long you have, so I started moving all those "someday" items further up the list. For example, we had been telling our friends that we would visit someday when the kids were older and it was easier to plan and we had more money. I was done waiting for someday. So I called them up on the Wednesday before Easter and asked what they were doing for the holiday. I stopped at the travel association and picked up a map on Thursday and on Friday we put the kids and the suitcases in the minivan and drove the 16 hours to my friends' house. I threw a cooler full of snacks and bread and a jar of peanut butter in the back of the minivan and when they were hungry we'd pull off the highway into a rest stop and we'd make sandwiches. We had a lovely visit with our friends and I'm glad that we went when we did. Aside from pushing myself outside of my comfort zone and proving to myself that I could take a leap, we also got to visit with our friends' mom and it ended up being our last chance because she died that summer. When my friends and I were in graduate school, she was the mom who had us all over to her house and fed us, so she had become another mother to me, too. Death always seems to come in threes, and that year I grieved for the loss of a baby, then a sister, then a mother.

This now-or-never mentality was still thick in the air, when on the last weekend of the summer I saw a notice for Godspell auditions in the church bulletin and I figured there was no time like the present. My parents had the soundtrack on cassette and we had listened to it countless times throughout my childhood while driving around in the wood-walled station wagon. I knew all the songs. We never put on musicals at my school growing up so I'd never really had the opportunity or even thought about doing anything theatrical, but I had sung in the school choir. I'd seen Godspell done at one of the local colleges though, and I always thought that show would be fun to do. I know it's not skydiving or world travel, but Godspell was on *my* bucket-list.

I walked around my house and daydreamed while I was cleaning, and I tried to remember the lyrics. I figured I'd sing *Day by Day* for the audition. We'd sung it in choir in high school and it was the classic song that everybody knows. But then as I washed the glass on the sliding doors, I looked out over my yard and while I looked at the setting sun I started singing the line from *By My Side* about where the horizon lies. (16) And I knew *that* was my song.

I printed out the lyrics so I could start to seriously practice and maybe not embarrass myself too badly, and I was surprised to find that I'd been hearing them wrong all those years. My entire life I had been singing "I condemn myself." I never realized that it said, "I can dare myself." And I certainly would have to dare myself to get up there and audition. At this point, I was still in awe that I could sing at all (never mind dance) now that I had my core muscles back after being in pain for all those years. I was used to being in pain, used to condemning myself and just accepting the suffering. I could always connect with the Sorrowful Mysteries and reflect on the sufferings of Jesus. The lives of the martyrs always made sense to me. But this new lyric really challenged me to stretch my understanding. Maybe I could take another leap of faith. (16)

I went to the audition and I waited outside in the gathering space. There was a mother and daughter next to me in the chairs and at first I thought they were working on a crossword puzzle together because they kept naming shows and characters and songs. Then I realized that they were filling in the same paper that

I was! I had just written "I sang in the folk group at church and in the choir in high school, and I was a worship-leader in the Christian club in college," and I was done with my list of musical credentials. They were listing all the different roles that she had played over the years. And she was half my age! I felt a little out of my league. When it was my turn to get called up, it turned out that I had to sing *a cappella*, all by myself, standing there on the altar, with my pastor and the music director sitting there staring at me. They waited. I tried to melt into the floor. I wanted to disappear. It didn't work. It was time to dare myself. Besides, I guessed the quickest way to be excused would be to just sing the song. So I did it.

I was so proud of myself for just finding the courage to audition. I had dared myself. I had survived it. Then the phone rang. Since I usually got calls from clients, I was in the habit of taking notes in my log during phone calls, and so I still have the exact quote from that call. It was the music director and she said that my "whole being" *was* that song. They asked if I would be in the show. It kind of worked out that I knew so little about theater because if I'd known at the time how much of a huge commitment it was I would have said that I couldn't make it work for my family. But I wasn't really analyzing and making plans anymore, I was allowing myself to be led by the spirit, and I was practicing trusting God to plan even better things than I could dream up for myself. Then, at the first rehearsal, the director called me aside because she wanted to be sure that I knew which character I would have to play. I hadn't quite thought about the fact that the show is an ensemble cast which means that I would have to sing every song, and dance every number, but then each character has a signature song. She wanted to know if I was okay with standing up in front of my community and *being* Mary Magdalene.

Things to think about:

- Learn to follow your gut reactions. Pay attention to what happens when you go against that inner knowing and choose something that you think you are supposed to do or that is expected of you.

- Picture your future self. Journal about your goals and your dreams for the future. Pay attention so that when something from your vision appears on your path, you are ready to embrace and accept it. If you feel like you missed an opportunity, don't worry, it will come back again in a new way on another turn of the spiral.

- Are there any challenges or obstacles in your life that you can reframe as opportunities for growth?

- What hopes and dreams do you have for your children? Do they help you to create opportunities for your child to explore or do they keep you from discovering who they are really meant to be?

- What is on your Someday list? What are the things that might need to rise to the top of your now-or-never list? What are you afraid of missing out on?

- What grief have you been holding on to that may need to be released? Are you holding any grudges? How much energy are you still using to maintain that grudge? Is the resentment serving you or is it weighing on you?

- Think of where you can send some forgiveness. Do you need to forgive someone else? Do you need to forgive any younger versions of yourself? Try thinking of the age that you were at the time, and look at a child that age and picture what they need. Send your child self some love and understanding.

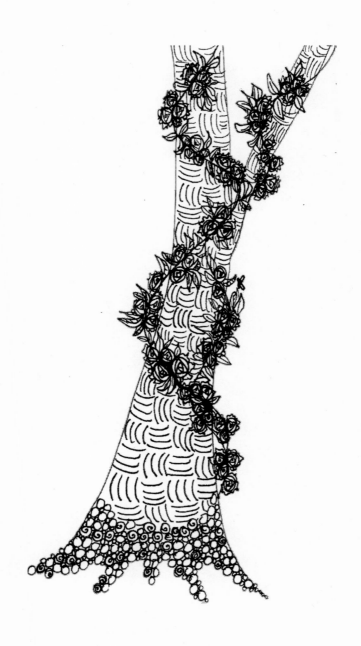

Chapter 4: Getting to the Heart of the Matter

The fourth energy center lies right in the center, above the 3 lower chakras, and below the 3 upper chakras. Through chakras 1, 2 and 3 we ground, we find our place in our family and our culture and our peer groups. Chakras 5, 6 and 7 embody how we connect with others through our expressions and our creations. At those higher vibrations, we connect to spirit, to universe, and to God. At the center, we balance. This is also where we feel our heart connection to others through relationships. We need to think about how much of our energy we use to focus on fulfilling our soul purpose, and how much of ourselves we give away to others. Let's get to the heart of the matter.

In addition to the heart center, the fourth chakra also involves our lungs and our breasts. Many of us have become accustomed to taking shallow breaths, running to keep busy so that we "can't catch our breath" instead of living for moments that "take our breath away." We need to slow down, and find time to sit and take deep breaths. We need to let out the toxins and breath in good, fresh air. We need to take care of each other, but we also need to refill the pitcher. We can't just keep going until something huge comes along and we "get the wind knocked out of us," or "we lose the wind from our sails." There are also so many expressions about milk from the breast to represent an endless supply of goodness. We give and we give and we keep making more. Some women give so much of themselves that they are completely drained. Sadness, anger, bitterness and fear can settle into our lungs or our breasts or clog our arteries until we cannot give any more away. (14)

In addition to finding balance in who we are, and where we are, we also need to balance ourselves between the past and the future so that we can bring more of our energy to the present moment. We often spend a lot of our energy reflecting on the past and dreaming of the future. Visualizations are powerful tools to help us focus towards our goals, but we can only create and make choices in the present. In this moment, we can say "yes, please" to what is calling to us and aligns with our vision, and say "no, thank you" to what drains us and doesn't serve our highest good. Worrying sends too much energy into the future. Focusing only on our regrets and what we wish we had done keeps us trapped in the past. Life travels in a spiral, not a straight line, so if you missed that opportunity last time, don't obsess over it. If you wish you had taken that chance, learn from that feeling and open your eyes and look for similar opportunities and catch them this next time around. You can think of it like that merry-go-round at the playground that you need to push as you run around gaining speed and then you jump on when the moment is just right. Maybe someone else has done the pushing and the ride is already going around with a bunch of smiling kids on it, and you just need to look for your opportunity to join. You can take a few turns to get your timing right, pay attention to how it moves, plan your strategy, and then when there is another opening, jump on and enjoy the ride.

Finding balance gives us the energy that we need to enjoy today. Parenting gives us many opportunities to practice this and to see how we are doing. It's easy to get lost in daydreams of when our kids will grow up and be wildly successful or we can be shocked that they grew-again! While it is okay to be amazed that they used to be so tiny and kind of toot our own horn for a second because it is has been really hard work feeding them six times a day for the last decade without even missing a single day, we can't get so lost in reflection that we cannot see them for who they are today. We need to be able to appreciate each phase and each stage. Try to just sit in that 4th grade orchestra concert and be really impressed with their current attempts. Sure, picturing where they will be in a few years if they keep practicing can make it more tolerable, but try not to miss this. Celebrate this moment with this kid. If you have multiple kids, you need to balance this with the needs of the others. You need to congratulate the one while consoling the other one who didn't get to perform, while entertaining the one who is bored, and try not to miss the entire concert while you're in the bathroom cleaning up something unpleasant. I share this because sometimes as a mom when we read something about being present and appreciating the moment, we can just picture the person who wrote that having the privilege of feeling one emotion at a time. But we can celebrate our mom-moments with even more pride because they are messy and real and complicated and even more beautiful because of that, not in spite of it.

◆

I often get asked how I get so many things done. I've had other moms actually use the excuse of having to do laundry to avoid volunteering or hanging out with friends once a month. My big secret to getting the laundry done is that I have modern conveniences and various electronic helpers. I think sometimes we forget to count our blessings. I put my laundry in a machine, I push the button, and then I walk away and get other things done. I can work on my computer, make phone calls, and write or go do something with my family. I can even leave the house and go to appointments or drive the kids to activities. And then later on when I have another quiet moment, I throw the clothes in the dryer and walk away again. When it comes time to fold the clothes though I have to be more physically present, but mentally it does not take a lot of concentration because I've been doing this since I was a kid, so I can do this task from muscle memory while my mind is working on some other project. If I'm tired of doing all of the thinking, I can treat myself to an episode of a favorite TV show or listen to a lecture so that I am being inspired or learning something new while I get my household tasks done. I've started to plan my day so that my appointments and classes are scheduled so that my favorite radio shows are on while I'm driving in the car. I remember when I was a kid and one of my grandmother's soap operas was broadcast over the radio as well as on TV so we could listen to it on the way to the grocery store. Now, with the abundance of technology, we don't even need to do that much planning, we can just play a recording. But I still like to catch some shows when they are live.

I don't think the details are as important as the intention. We need to find balance so that all of our busyness becomes a blessing instead of a burden. We need to remember to be grateful for the piles of clothes because it means that we have enough. We actually have way too many with all the hand-me-downs. I think the youngest owns 36 pairs of pants! And I'd hate to count the long sleeve and short sleeve shirts and sweatshirts. All this abundance (picture huge piles of dirty laundry here) means that we have people to take care of and to love. Sometimes when we feel buried under the sheer volume of things that we are expected to do, it is hard to remember to see the blessings. But if we find balance, then we can appreciate being in the moment a little more. If folding clothes means that I get to sit down, slow down, and enjoy a favorite movie without any guilt, then I can appreciate the moment. If I'm feeling really generous, I could even have a quiet moment where I actually notice each item of clothing and send love and gratitude to the person who gave it to us. I can remember the time when my kid wore that t-shirt, and appreciate the kid that they are today, because soon enough it will be too small. Maybe someday we'll have all this extra time because they'll finally learn to wipe their hands on a napkin instead of on their t-shirts and we won't have to treat each stain, but by then we'll need to spend that time talking about their relationships or choosing a major as they apply to colleges. So for now, we can choose the more positive thought in the moment, and choose positive people to listen to for encouragement, as we continue to multi-task and pretend that we've got this all figured out.

We also need to remember that we are never too busy to reach out and help others, and we can't get so overwhelmed that we use our work or our household responsibilities as an excuse to never go out into our communities. When my family volunteers together, that is what creates our community and our connections and our network of support. We give back to the community that has been here for us, and that we know will be here if anything catastrophic ever happens. On those days, we do activities that may not seem fun, like sorting bottles or shoveling horse-poop or painting fences, and we make it a fun day together. Many of these days include potluck meals and conversation with other families, as well as fresh air and time away from our electronics. Taking time to volunteer doesn't take something away from our family; it is how we refill our pitcher.

◆

A few months after performing in Godspell, I found myself on a bus to New York City. When my friend invited me to her graduation, my first thought was that of course I couldn't go. Leaving my kids always took so much planning and then was even more work when I got home because they would miss me and then be clingy. They would push the envelope with crazy behaviors to fight for extra attention once I was home. It's nice to feel needed, but it can also feel like you are being punished anytime you try to do something for yourself and not just for them, even though a little time away may be what keeps mommy sane enough to continue to do this job. So I was always running these cost-benefit analyses in my head. How much would I really need to pay and was it worth it? But when I actually sat down and looked at the situation to see if I could visualize making it happen, I was surprised to find that I didn't really have babies anymore. Even the baby of the family had weaned and I could finally travel without a breast pump and bottles. And though New York City seems like it is on an entirely different planet than where I exist, I could actually get there by bus. The bus would take me just a few blocks away from where they were having the ceremony, I could go out to dinner with everyone afterwards, and be home to sleep in my own bed and have nighttime snuggles with the little one.

I had just re-connected with this woman online because we were reading the same books and were passionate about the same issues. It wasn't really hard to believe because she was one of my big sisters from my sorority, but it was a nice surprise to find someone posting things on social media that really resonated with me. We started sending messages online and talked on the phone. One day she asked me what I did for my own pleasure. I can still remember the visceral feeling that I had upon hearing the word "pleasure." Just listening to her say that word made me uncomfortable and I kind of looked around to make sure nobody was listening. I was home alone and we were on the phone so we were safe, but thank goodness we weren't at a coffee shop where someone might overhear. I'm well trained by my years in school to think of answers on command, but in this moment I had no answer. I couldn't even think on those terms. For so long I had done what was expected, what I was supposed to do, what would make others happy or what would keep me safe. I didn't ever think of doing something just for my own pleasure and now that she asked, that kind of bothered me. My friend was in the mastery program with Mama Gena's School of Womanly Arts in NYC and the women would connect regularly online from all over the world and then this was their big gathering with everyone flying in for the graduation. (17) Apparently I was not alone in needing to find a sisterhood to help me reconnect with what I was really passionate about and what brought me joy.

Growing up in a male-dominated society, to play it safe, many women hide all the parts of ourselves that are feminine. Maybe we liked pretty dresses when we were little, but now we only wear dress pants and button down shirts to work, which is just a slightly feminine version of the man's standard outfit. We take the birth control pill and use pain medications when we have our periods so that we can just keep pretending that every day of the month is the same. We are told that tuning in to our intuition is a "soft skill." We are told that being emotional is a weakness. So this was amazing to meet other women who were finding ways to reclaim their natural gifts and learning to tune in to their inner knowing and acknowledge their superpowers.

As I sat in the audience waiting for the event to start, I knew that just being in that room was such a huge accomplishment for me. To give it an extra dose of perspective and make sure that I was paying attention, I ended up sitting next to this woman who looked exactly like a shy, quiet, younger version of me. I loved sitting next to her, feeling her try to shrink and hide, and it gave me a marker for how far I'd come. Much of what they did at that event was way outside of my comfort zone, but instead of thinking that there must be something wrong with me, I felt happy that all these women had found what they needed on their journey towards healing. Some of the women there had needed to find their courage and stand in their power to leave dangerous relationships or the wrong job or to rid their bodies of cancer. They were wearing their independence and their healthy bodies triumphantly. I had come a long way, but I was still very shy compared to these women, and anyone who knew me in my regular everyday life would be shocked to see me there. The one person that I feel like I could've shared this with was my sister-in-law. When I walked in, there was a whole group of ladies wearing hot-pink feather boas and glitter which reminded me of her wedding day, so I knew that she was there with me in spirit.

Sitting there made me think of all the ways in which I still hide. I know that I do it out of habit to help me to feel safe. Being criticized triggers something in our ancient DNA that sets off alarms warning us that we'll be ostracized and kicked out of the tribe and that we won't be able to survive out on our own. We feel the fear as strongly as we did when we still lived in caves and hunted woolly mammoth. And even though we live in a really diverse, global community connected by a web of technology now, we still feel this primal need to fit in and be accepted. And despite all the videos and other evidence to prove to us that there isn't a single right way to live, there are still so many people who will defend their narrow image of the world with their lives.

So how much do we come out into the light and how much do we hide? Whenever my friends come out to me about their preferences for relationships or the secret career that they always dreamed about but that their family didn't support, I am never really surprised. I think that our friends can already see what we don't really want to admit to ourselves. They already know and they already like us anyway. I let my friends share their news in their own time, but I wouldn't say that I'm really shocked very often. So, I pictured my own coming out. I pictured everyone finding out that all this time, while I was pregnant and breastfeeding, that I was in fact, a woman. It seemed a ridiculous thing to try to hide. But I still felt scared if anyone talked about it too loudly. I would go to my women's circle and share my birth story and that was fine, but then it was really awkward if someone at the office asked me if I had a vaginal birth. When they mentioned that I had a vagina really loudly in a public place, I could already feel the infection setting in and on the car ride home I felt the stabs of physical pain starting as I held the fear in my abdomen.

One day I was going to pick up my kids from summer camp and it was way too hot out to wear pants, so I put on a sundress and a wide-brimmed hat to keep from getting sunburned. As I walked across the field with my dress swishing, I was very conscious of how feminine I looked and I became hyper-aware of my surroundings and I felt my body go into survival mode. They say that we are the descendants of the women that they couldn't burn. But we can still feel in our bones that it is dangerous to be seen as a strong woman. It is not safe to speak out or to stand out in a crowd. We remember the burning times in our DNA and in our collective memories.

While I was on that bus to New York City I was reading a book that I'd picked up at my favorite used bookstore. I like to walk through the store looking for something to catch my eye until I feel which book is calling to me. I find the best things that way. Finding myself on my own kind of pilgrimage, I loved the synchronicity of reading *Crossing to Avalon: A Woman's Midlife Quest for the Sacred Feminine* while I was on the trip. (18) I had loved *The Mists of Avalon* when it was on TV and then I had listened to the book on CDs while I commuted to the university, and then I had read the hardcover. (19) So I was quite familiar with the imagery and the symbols that Jean Shinoda Bolen used in *Crossing to Avalon*. She similarly shed light on the feminine aspects of the grail legends as she shared her story of self-discovery through the realm of the Goddess. When Bolen wrote about the magical child archetype and how women often dream of giving birth to a special child, but the dream is really about fulfilling their personal destiny, it sounded a lot like the dreams I had about my daughter Magdalena. (Bolen, p.16) So many other things that she said in her book confirmed the truths that I felt when I wrote my first book. And I was reading it while journeying to discover the sacred feminine with some "Sister Goddesses" and share with them how far I had come on my own journey of healing.

Reading her book while traveling on this one-day pilgrimage gave me the fuel that I needed to continue my work. It is easy to get discouraged when you put yourself out there and encounter the critics. One woman in my doula group told me that it was nice that I wrote to "get it off my chest," but that she didn't see any value in sharing our stories in books. But I was currently getting a lot out of reading Bolen's memoir, and she also said that authors are the modern day shamans who have visions for their tribe. (Bolen, p.36) Bolen said that hearing someone tell the truth of their own lives can sustain another person on her own journey. (p.266) She said, "sometimes a person needs a story more than food to stay alive." (p.273) As even more confirmation that I had found this book for a reason, she kept mentioning how our journey is not a straight line; it spirals.

Similar to my own discoveries, Bolen also talked a lot about mothering and birth as an initiating experience for women. She said, "For me, pregnancy was an initiating experience that changed my body, shifted my consciousness, taught me surrender, and was the beginning of the dawning awareness of the physical, psychological, and spiritual demands and gifts that would come through being a mother." (Bolen, p.194) She talks about how everyone is excited to meet the new person who is being born, but that it is equally important to acknowledge who the woman will become as a result of this experience. Like another kind of birth, she speaks to the courage that it takes to overcome our fear of being seen, of standing out, and of speaking our truth as we bring forth what we know. (18)

Bolen also spoke of the importance of women's circles as a place where we can act as midwife for each other and hold space for each woman to step fully into her true self. She mentions how mothering is often another way for us to give nurturing to others, when what we need is to learn to receive and to be nurtured. One day, when meeting with my doula over a cup of tea, we had talked about all of the things that were missing in our modern, busy community. I wrote a list of all the things that we could do if we gathered in a monthly women's circle. It included things like taking time for deep breathing, telling stories, creating art, nurturing each other, sharing a meal, and sharing our wisdom. I envisioned a circle that includes women from all different ages and backgrounds. I was tired of only finding groups for one subgroup. There were groups for women with preschoolers, or working women, or young professionals etc. What if you made friends within that group and were just starting to feel at home and then you didn't have a preschooler anymore (because they tend to grow out of that quickly)? Would you then just get kicked out of the group? Do you have to stop attending your young professionals networking group because you had another birthday? It always seemed wrong in a way. I also loved that Bolen seemed to share my vision of the importance of women's circles as sacred space and not just as a networking group. She confirmed my suspicions that women sharing their stories is healing. I also love the synchronicity that it was on this quest that I met the woman who would illuminate the next path to take on my journey. (18)

In the opening scene of the musical Godspell, I looked up to the stained glass window in my church, and while staring at the circular mandala pattern (partly for inspiration and partly to avoid seeing the audience staring at me), I spoke Marianne Williamson's words: "Our Deepest Fear is not that we are inadequate. Our deepest fear is that we are powerful beyond measure." The words of her famous poem were adapted to fit into the litany of philosopher's quotes that are woven together into the Tower of Babel prologue in the updated version of the show. When all of the voices were fighting to be heard above the crowd, I just kept reiterating the idea that we are born to make manifest the Glory of God. (20)

I know that each time I step outside of my comfort zone and I own a little more of my power, that I am not only breaking patterns for my own daughter and modeling that for my sons, but I am giving other women permission to let themselves shine. Seeing the women shine that day in New York City was a huge inspiration for me, but I also know that the types of activities that they were doing that day were way too far outside the cultural norm for many women who were brought up to be neither seen nor heard. Since I have now been a part of both of those worlds, I have tried to become a bridge between the two. I try to show other women how we can find easy, accessible ways to start taking some baby steps towards being our true selves. We can take small steps towards the things that are calling to us, the things that we would love to try, and we just need to get over the newness and the discomfort. Sometimes we need to push past our feelings of guilt and shame and give ourselves permission to try. We need to notice and acknowledge when we are having a really strong reaction to something in particular. Sometimes when we are rejecting something or feeling jealous of others, those feelings are really pointing us towards something that we want but we can't even admit it to ourselves.

Every once in a while, Spirit calls us to take a bigger leap of faith. Musicals may not be your thing, so you'll need to pay attention to what is calling to you, but performing in Godspell had given me the perfect chance to take that leap. Singing and dancing in front of my community was a huge stretch for me and took all of my courage and some special tea (liquid courage) at intermission to help me to finally express myself fully. This was music that I'd known since childhood, with a message I really believed in, performed in my own church with an encouraging group of people there to support me the entire way. It didn't hurt that in theatre, you have the ability to hide in plain sight. I could sing and dance (which I had secretly always wanted to do and just never had enough opportunities when I was younger) but I could blame it on the director and choreographer who told me to do it. I wore a bright colored dress that swooshed elegantly when I danced, but it was a costume, so nobody could judge me or tell me that it was wrong somehow. I could also be really spiritual and emotional and finally be my full self but disguise it as entertainment.

It is so healing when you allow yourself to follow your own passions. Yours may not be singing or dancing or writing. It may be that you love to play sports, but you feel that you are too old. Maybe you used to run but now you feel like you'll never get back into shape or you don't have enough time with all of your responsibilities. Maybe you really want to play with your kids on the playground, but you feel like moms are supposed to sit on the sidelines. Maybe you would love to coach Little League, but you let your husband do it instead. Maybe you don't think it is proper to wear pretty dresses or have long hair or whatever else at a certain age. Maybe you always wanted to be an engineer, but you were told that path wasn't for you. Sometimes, I see moms who think that it is too late to follow their dreams, so they sign up their kids instead. I see dads who push their kids to be the athlete that they wish they had become. I see parents encourage their children to take the career path that they had really wanted, but they think that it is too late to start over. But it is not their dream, their passion, or their

objection handling (girl scout cookies example)

path, so it will never work. As parents, it is important to nurture our children and help them to discover and develop their natural gifts. We can help to create opportunities for our children to follow their dreams, but we also need to be aware of our own dreams, and pay attention to the opportunities that are put in our path. Sometimes it may not be the right season, but it is never too late.

You can start to tune back in to your true self by looking for ways in which you give too much of your power away to external sources, or to some authority instead of listening to your own inner guidance. That is what your passion or your desires really are, like your gifts and talents, they are uniquely yours. Take something that seems sort of simple on the surface and is not heavy with belief systems and family obligations, and look at how many ways we are told what to think. Just for an example, bring your awareness to fashion trends, and how we are told which colors are in style this year. Even our furniture and the paint colors on our walls go in and out of fashion. Certain foods are popular and then fade away as another trend takes over. We are surrounded by these marketing messages and product placement, but at the same time many of us don't believe that we deserve to have the latest thing. We wait and buy it on clearance. We feel behind the times, always trying to catch up or feeling like we'll never get ahead. We constantly feel like we aren't good enough. Some people reject all things new and hate change. Other people won't wear the same thing twice and are always on to the next thing and can't stay in one place for long. Maybe what they really desire is to find something that feels like home, and they've never found it. We often get caught up with looking over the picket fence and thinking it is greener on their side, when we actually have no idea what it really feels like to be over there. The people on that side of the fence are probably sick of feeling like they do and think that our lives look easier from a distance. Let's start by figuring out what our own feelings are and then let others do the same.

You could start with something like changing your wardrobe to start tuning in to your inner knowing, which is more affordable and attainable and a lot easier than renovating your house or making a whole career change. Start to say "yes" to the outfit that draws your eye when you first walk into the store. Listen to how your internal dialog starts to talk you out of it. Maybe this time, when you first look at that pretty shirt, you can actually stop and pick it up and feel the fabric between your fingers, and maybe even go and try it on.

Even if you don't buy it when it is full price, notice and acknowledge your desire and give yourself permission to picture yourself wearing it. Learn to calculate the true cost of going against your intuition. Usually when I talk myself out of the one pretty shirt, I buy three plain ones instead. Bypassing my first instinct ends up costing even more and will never give me that same feeling that I would have had if I had just followed my heart.

Create a new habit and try on the pretty outfit and see how you feel in it before you even look at the price. See if you can picture an event where you would wear it. I just bought a dress that was way too fancy for my normal mom-life and I was afraid that I would have nowhere to wear it and it would just sit in my closet with the tags on, but I let myself visualize the type of people who would appreciate it, and the type of event where it would be perfect. When I said "yes" and paid for it, the invitation to exactly that kind of party was waiting for me when I got home. It is fun to visualize a better life, but it is even sweeter when you allow the universe to deliver. When you take notice and say thank you for the small gifts, more will start to arrive. Start to allow yourself to have these small moments, and soon the synchronicities won't even surprise you anymore and you will start to get a glimpse into how you too, are powerful beyond measure.

If fashion is not your thing or is too emotional for you (maybe you were picked on too much at school and you are not ready to go there yet) try something else. You can practice choosing what you feel like eating while you are still in the car on the way to the restaurant or the store. Ask your body what it needs and then see what pops into your head first. If that sounds crazy, just think about what you are in the mood to eat. What have you been craving? Picture that food (turkey sandwich on a fancy roll) or a few ingredients (I'd love something with goat cheese and sun-dried tomatoes) and then when you get to the restaurant look for that on the menu. Decide what looks good before you look at the price. Give yourself permission to give your body what it is craving. If you are getting more daring, you can ask the server whether they can make that particular sandwich for you without even looking at the menu. Ask them to make you that turkey sandwich with goat cheese and sun-dried tomatoes on a fancy roll. And then get really bold and ask for the sweet potato fries instead of the regular fries. Feel free to alter this story and substitute whatever food makes you happy. Or dare yourself to try the special, ask the server to suggest something or try something completely new.

The trick is to tune in to what you always really wanted, and not what you think is the right answer. We have so many things that we have been taught, and we need to start to sift through and see which lessons are helpful and aligned with our core beliefs, and which no longer serve us. Be gentle with yourself at this phase, because your true self might be buried kind of deep beneath all the layers of what you have been told that you should do and how you have been told that you should think. Maybe you would like to try something new, but you always go with what is safe and get something that you know you'll like. Maybe you have been taught not to waste money and not to waste food. Give yourself permission to do this research, and know that it will not mean that you will become wasteful. How much money can you gamble? What if you get it and you hate it? It's going to be okay. Now you have new information. You are only out a few dollars. You are not hurting anyone. You need to stop beating yourself up. You can start with a sandwich. Give yourself permission to risk asking this much of the universe.

It is amazing how much you can punish yourself

over every little thing. You need to stop this merry-go-round sometime, so that you can then turn around and try it another way. You need to bring your stress response and that internal dialog a little closer into alignment with your current reality. You need to understand that your epigenetics has wired you to respond to your ancestors' environment, and you just don't live like that today. You can appreciate that these responses are normal and natural, and that the gut reaction was put there for a reason, but then learn to pull yourself more quickly back into the present moment. Maybe when you look at those weird ingredients on the menu, you can start to feel your ancestors telling you not to risk it, to just be safe and go with what you know. Maybe they lived through a famine or the Great Depression, but when you hear that whisper you need to remind yourself that you currently have a huge supermarket full of food to choose from and enough money to eat again later. Maybe when you try the new sandwich and you don't like it and you start to think about not finishing it, you can hear your mother telling you to clean your plate or you can see those starving children on that TV commercial and the guilt is stronger than your desire. The trick is to find your own balance as you learn to turn down the volume on all of those other voices so that you can start to hear yourself again.

The 4th chakra is where you learn to tune in to your heart's desire, but on the other hand, it is also where you may find some woundings around love and relationships. Often this shows up as an imbalance. Maybe you are in one or more relationships that do not feel balanced. Maybe you keep giving and giving in hopes that someday they'll reciprocate. If you are really good at giving of yourself, maybe you find that you keep attracting takers. Sometimes, like with raising children, we know that they can't take care of us the way that we take care of them. We are the nurturer in this relationship, but when they accept what we give with an open heart, in return it feeds our souls. Parents need nurturing too, but they need to get that from another relationship. You need to find people who let you be vulnerable and places where you feel like you can be taken care of and you can really relax. You need some moments that refill your own pitcher, so that you can continue to give to others. They say that you can't pour from an empty cup. So many women keep giving and giving and never find ways or make the time to recharge their energy. Women are taught to believe that they don't deserve to take time for themselves, to be served instead of always serving, and our whole society suffers because these women are running on empty. Caroline Myss thinks that this is the root cause of our epidemic of breast cancer. (14) We try to nurture the whole world, but we don't know how to receive. Some women seem to do everything for their community, they volunteer and they serve and they take care of everyone, until they suddenly die too young because they have nothing left to give. It just happened to a mother in my community, and once again, everyone said that they were shocked and that they just couldn't believe it.

In our Hollywood romance culture, we are taught from a young age that we need to look for our better half. We find someone who understands us and whose puzzle piece fits with our own (because we have matching or mirroring wounds) and we cling to each other. I looked for that fairy tale romance and I was so thankful when I found it so that we could get married and live happily ever after. I didn't learn until after how that model can make it harder when you want to start healing those wounds. It would be more ideal to have two healthy and whole adults who love and support each other. But we are sold on this romanticized model of a victim and a rescuer. Either the helpless princess is saved by her knight or the rebel bad boy is fixed by the good girl. Sometimes they take turns saving each other. There is a great strategy game called "Royal

Rescue" that you can get for your kids which seems progressive because they set it up so that half of the time the princess gets to save the knight. (21) But what if your "better half" starts to heal and throws off the whole balance of the relationship? If one of those half-persons now feels more fully themselves it can feel like they are taking up more than half, maybe just 60%, but does that mean that their partner needs to get smaller to make room? What if they could both grow and become a power couple? We can get defensive when we feel like someone is pushing into our space. As a part of a couple, we have to learn to do this dance. We need to learn to keep coming back to center. Unfortunately though, we often retreat to our comfort zone right when we are on the verge of a big transformation because it is really uncomfortable to lean that far off center. Maybe letting go so that you can both grow into fully-realized individuals would be healthier, but letting go is not easy to do.

One day (when they weren't babies anymore) we took all the kids for some family fun, and went snow tubing at the local ski mountain. We were on the big conveyer belt that drags you back up to the top, when suddenly we saw a little girl who leaned too far over and her handle disconnected. Her tube started plummeting down the hill. It was picking up speed. The staff was calling to her and telling her to just let go. If she rolled out of the tube she would be better off. But she clung to the safety of that tube with a white-knuckled death grip. When we are stressed and scared, we freeze. We've all had those dreams (or real-life moments) where you know that you need to run but your legs won't move. When her tube inevitably hit into the other people below her at full speed there was a lot of collateral damage. I often think of her when life gives me those moments when every part of my being knows that I need to just let go, but I can't do it. I stay in jobs longer than I should. I stay in relationships longer than I should. I usually stay at parties and have one more drink than I should. Cutting ties and breaking habits is not easy.

We can find this need to let go in our friendships and our business relationships too, not just in our romantic relationships. I had been working with a business partner for a few years so that we could share the load and say "yes" to more opportunities. I had met him in my entrepreneurs networking group and we were both passionate about education and helping people. As a busy mom it worked well for me logistically to team up with him on some projects because his time was so much more flexible than mine. I could work a lot from home and he could take any client appointments that conflicted with my kids' activities. I would prepare the plans and the materials, and then he could get there early and start teaching the class, and I'd get there after I put the kids on the bus. I thought that my hard work and dedication would pay off, and I thought that I could make him see my value, but I felt disrespected on a number of occasions. We spent a lot of time together working on projects with clients and with our interns and students, but I started to feel like he enjoyed my company more than he actually valued my work, and he started to cross the line. I tried to find ways to professionally map out a new business model where we could work separately, but I didn't want to burn any bridges. Despite all those nagging feelings and warning signs, I finally had to just break it off completely when he disrespected me in front of the students and embarrassed me in front of a client. I felt like a failure because I wasn't able to come up with a strategy or find the right words that would make it all better, but I finally realized that I could not change him or fix him, so I needed to walk away.

Instead of focusing on how I had just lost all those clients (and interns and students) and walked away from the projects in which I had invested so much time and energy, I was trying to be positive about how I suddenly had some extra time on my hands. While I recalibrated my schedule and reevaluated my plans, I caught up on some gardening projects. I had this rose bush that had grown up around a tree and was strangling its branches. I should have pruned it much sooner. When I saw it spring up as a young rosebush though, I only thought of how I loved to smell the blossoms and how the rose hips were good for tea. Now it had become overgrown. I got my clippers and I went to work. There were dead vines and dead branches all intertwined with the newer growth. Sometimes, when you try to cut away the dead, you end up cutting out a lot of green branches, too. With all those thorns grabbing at your skin and pricking your fingers and catching in your hair, it is just too painful to untangle them. At that point you just need to cut it off at the base and haul it out in one big mess and then see what you have left to work with. Similarly, after those drastic prunings in our relationships, we need to let it rest for the winter and see what comes back in the spring.

In my business partnership, I saw the problems starting when they were small. I knew when it first took root that it would continue to grow if I did not take action right away, but I thought that I could handle it. I thought the benefits still outweighed the prick of the thorns. But then I started to see where failing to speak up had let those habits grow. The vines grew slowly and quietly until they were choking out the very tree that was supporting them as they reached for the sky. I started to see the long-term costs of continuing to work with someone who did not respect me, but I did not know how to untangle myself without getting bloodied and battered in the process. And even if I managed to walk away, would there be thorns stuck in my jeans, unseen but waiting to scratch me again the next time I put them on, as little reminders of how I should have known better? I needed to stop looking for someone else to acknowledge me and to appreciate all of my hard work. I had outgrown the partnership and I needed to accept that they could not be happy for my growth, because it meant that I was growing away from them.

When you are ready to complete your caterpillar phase, you need to trust your instincts that the time is right to start building your cocoon. Your caterpillar friends may not be happy for you. They may say some pretty hurtful things. They may stop speaking to you entirely. You may not want to graduate from this phase, because you feel like you just got good at it. When you start off as a freshman everything is exciting and new, but also a little bit terrifying. By the time you are a senior, you are confident and you've got it all figured out. You are practically running the place. But then when you graduate, you are just stepping up to another level. They call it commencement because it is just a new beginning. All of a sudden you are in a new place, and you are starting over as a freshman, again. So maybe now that you are really good at being a caterpillar you feel like you'd like to stay there a little bit longer. It is hard to let go. It is hard to start again and be brand new and not have any clue. You don't know how to fly. What is it like to have wings? To transform, you need to die to self first. You need to cut away the dead and the overgrown. You need to let go. You need to trust. You need to take that leap of faith, but first you need to go within and gather your strength, and start anew.

Things to think about:

- What percentage of your thoughts and energy do you spend on regret and worry?

- Are your relationships balanced? Do you feel supported or feel like you are falling? Are you leaning too far? How many parts of yourself have you given away?

- How balanced are you between your duty to family/ community/culture and your own passions/purpose?

- What are you passionate about? What is your soul-purpose?

- What are some things that you can try as you start to tune in to your inner knowing? Think of some easy ways to get started like with fashion, decorating, food, creative projects, or playing with your kids.

- What phase are you in? Are you ready to build your cocoon? Are you still growing? What resources do you need to gather before you can complete this phase?

Chapter 5: Express Yourself

The fifth energy center is all about personal expression, following your dreams and speaking up for yourself. It includes your throat and neck (not surprisingly where I carry my scars and tumors from when I was punished for speaking out) but it also includes your arms and your hands that you use to express yourself and to create things. With a healthy 5th chakra you can dance and sing and write and create art. If you have blocks in this energy center, you may have chronic sore throats, scoliosis, and swollen glands (all of which I had growing up) and other physical symptoms in the mouth, throat, and spine. (30) For energy to reach the fifth, you need to have healthy flow through your lower chakras, and feel secure and powerful enough to fully express yourself in the physical world. I think too many women don't feel like they have that kind of freedom of expression, and this is also why I keep hearing about more and more women with thyroid problems presenting at middle-age. (14) The throat chakra is where you take your mental ideas from the 6th chakra and the passionate emotions from the 4th and send them out into the world through your words and actions. When this becomes a matter of acculturated habits, and you listen to something other than your own intuition and your own soul-purpose, then you can develop physical symptoms in this part of your body.

Children at four years of age are often starting preschool or going to more playgroups and they need to learn healthy ways to express themselves and to let their feelings out, without hurting others or breaking things. This is a good time to start practicing building things and creating things and making sounds and music in new ways. As adults we can try to remember what our favorite activities were when we were four years old and maybe reconnect to our love of coloring or to just sing a song or write stories or plant flowers, and not because we are trading our skills for dollars, but just because it is fun. Sculpt something out of playdough with your kids, or make some pretzel dough together (with that bread machine that you received as a gift and never remember to use) and form different shapes with it before you bake it. At this age, the kids love to help in the kitchen and the garden and they are actually getting to where they can be helpful and not just distracting or putting everything in their mouths. You can use this creative phase in your mothering as an opportunity to spend quality time together with your child and to reconnect to your true nature.

◆

In the song *By My Side*, from Godspell, Mary Magdalene sings to Jesus and asks him where he's going and if he'll take her with him on the journey. (16) She wants to travel that road with him, wherever it may lead. She knows that he is not taking the easy path, and she puts a pebble in her shoe and shows him that she can still walk in spite of the pain, to prove that she can keep going, she can share the suffering. She calls the pebble "Dare" and it is carried until they both have had enough and then she takes it from her shoe when she is ready to walk the new road. Then, when she has found that new path, and the suffering is over, she can finally take His hand and truly be by His side. They are one in the spirit.

When I sang this song in the Godspell rehearsals, I often thought of that moment when I first saw Magdalena, not as my daughter after all, but as my true self. I remembered my vision in which she was across the river and I was trying to find the path that would lead me to a bridge that would connect me with her. I sang to my future self and wondered when we would become one. I still identified so strongly with my little girl, and although I did not want to play the victim anymore, I didn't know how to move forward without leaving her alone. I carried her with me like a heavy burden and I kept putting one foot in front of the other. I felt that pebble every time that the path was not easy and I had to find my courage. I showed up. I did the work. When life gave me assignments that challenged me, I thought of them as opportunities to grow into becoming more like that vision of her, and I would take the chance in those "Magdalena Moments." I would say "yes" and I would let the spirit lead me.

I had met a Sister Goddess on my pilgrimage who had invited me to a women's retreat that summer. When she sent me the link with the registration information, it was exactly what I had been seeking, but wouldn't have known to search for. It would be a chance to connect with the Earth through spending time camping in nature, but in a private setting with only women so I could really relax. They said that there would be nobody taking pictures and you could just be yourself and tune in to how you felt and not worry about how you looked. There were women facilitating workshops on different topics and you could join whichever ones sounded appealing. And they were going to feed me. For someone who is always planning and facilitating and care-giving and shopping and cooking and feeding, this was huge.

I registered and I packed and I anticipated being able to relax and be nourished and nurtured and maybe even sleep through the night for the first time in a decade. I dreamed of having enough quiet time to find an answer to the question about what brings me pleasure. Right before I left on the trip though, I had this encounter with a new real estate client that literally sickened me. I was seduced into helping him with promises of easily making thousands of dollars in commission. I ditched my kids to jump when he said jump and I followed the lead in hopes of the big payout. I told myself that with the money I could take my kids on a wonderful vacation that would more than make up for my missing the afternoon trip to the town pool.

Then, after I drove him around all afternoon looking at all of the available investment properties, the client dismissed me with a chilling look and pushed $30 into my hand "for gas," and patted me, and called me one of those condescending pet names that should not be used for a business professional. He made me feel small and insignificant. I felt sick. It was like a punch in the gut. I was really pissed off.

At this point, I had learned so much about how our emotions affect our physical health and I could feel the rage tightening up those lower chakras. I couldn't tell him how I really felt, and I had to be professional and walk away and pretend that it was fine, but I could already feel the anger infecting my bladder. What I didn't know was how to stop it. I was afraid to be sick on my trip, so I took a homeopathic remedy for urinary health and I drank cranberry juice and I even went to the doctor to get an antibiotic for my urinary tract infection. Nothing worked. It had gotten so bad that now I was bleeding when I went pee and I was in a huge amount of pain. Every time I remembered the look on my client's face when he suddenly changed his tune, I felt violated. I felt stupid for believing him. He had used me, and I had let him. I knew that I had let my fear about being able to provide for my family overtake my intuition. I hadn't listened to my gut.

By the time I got to the retreat, I was in so much pain that I was having trouble functioning. I have been camping since I was a kid and I'm a Girl Scout leader, but I had never set this particular tent up all by myself. I had already been moving slowly because of the pain, and now it was time for the group to gather under the main festival tent for the opening ceremony and I was still not done setting up my tent. Then this woman came over and offered to help. She wasn't one of the official volunteers; she just saw a need and offered to be a friend to me in that moment. Years later, I still remember how good it felt to set up the tent together. Never doubt yourself if you think that you have just provided a small service. It may have been huge to the person who needed to learn to receive in small ways before she could start to open up to more. You never know when you are planting a seed.

Having that new friend to walk with into the large gathering and find a seat together also made a huge difference. It was nice to not feel intimidated and alone even though I was surrounded by hundreds of strangers. As part of the opening remarks and reminders for the weekend, the organizers asked if there was anything that anyone needed in order to be able to fully enjoy their experience that weekend. I was so desperate at this point that I found my voice and overcame my fear of speaking out and I actually asked for help. I asked if anyone did energy healing. I had never been to an energy healing session before, and I kind of surprised myself when I asked for that. I had read about it, but I hadn't gotten up the courage to actually try it yet. I had felt the energy of that encounter settle into my bladder, and I believed that I just needed to learn how to let that go so that I could heal physically. In that moment, I met my teacher.

I didn't know it then, but looking back later I was thankful for the infection that taught me to listen to my intuition and that led me to the person who could teach me how to remove those negative energies from my body (or remove the blocks so that my energy could flow and restore my physical health.) As soon as she sat with me and asked for permission to tune in to my story, she started asking about who had pissed me off. And then she asked me about my relationship with my mother. Then she asked for permission to help my body remove the residual anesthesia from my tissues, when I hadn't even told her that I had recently had surgeries. Lying down on that blanket with her sitting beside me, I let myself be taken care of and I started to feel the physical pain release and fade away as my tissues and organs let go of the emotional hurt. I surrendered, I received, and I was given the gift of a beautiful weekend that I will always remember.

The first session that I went to on that retreat was a Grief Ritual. It was from an entirely different tradition than what I am used to from my own Catholic upbringing, but I found that many of the rituals had similar roots. We used ashes and water and incense. We sang and lit candles and had a fire. There are similarities and differences between all the traditions, but I think that we all share an underlying human need for ceremony. I think that in our busy modern culture and especially in the western world, there is not enough ceremony. We don't give ourselves enough time for grieving or for celebrating. With my Girl Scouts, every time they mark the passage from one level to the next, I have them light a candle and reflect on where they've been and what they've learned and then they set intentions for the next part of their journey. They do something similar in my kids' Tae Kwon Do school when they complete working on one belt level and are pausing to reflect before receiving their next belt. Then, before they put on the new belt, they visualize what they will work on while wearing that belt color, and they speak their promises into the belt and to their future self that they will take the steps necessary to work towards realizing that vision. I think we waste too much energy arguing about what is the correct ritual. You can stick to the rituals that your family or your organization is familiar with, or you can work together and create new ceremonies, but the important thing is not to let the moment pass without pausing and honoring the passage.

At the grief ceremony I was able to finally give myself the time that I needed to finish my own grieving. I made a little assemblage of tokens that I gathered from nature. As I walked in the woods I picked up things that called to me as I thought of each loss and I found beautiful things for the baby, the sister and the mother that had passed away that year. Although I would often push my own grief aside, because others were clearly hurting more, I still needed to give myself permission to feel and to release my own pain. And as I let myself sink into the deep grieving, I found that it wasn't just the unexpressed sadness that I was holding while I was busy taking care of everyone else. I was holding on to *everything* too tightly. My fear caused me to clench my fists and hold on tighter even though that hurt. I needed to let go. I needed to stop trying to control everything. I needed to stop trying to fix everything. I needed to stop thinking that I had to save the whole world all by myself. I could find friends and together we could each do our piece.

That night, I couldn't fall into a deep sleep after all. I enjoyed a nice walk in the moonlight with a porcupine of all things. And the next day I went to a session with my new Goddess friend and I learned how to embrace my sensual femininity. We put aside what was not aligned with our most fabulous self, and we invited loveliness into our bubble. Then, I went to a workshop where I let go of the stories that no longer served me and I held other women as they learned to let go as well. That night I danced around a huge bonfire to the primal beat of the drums. I had been a huge fan of the *Earth's Children* series by Jean M. Auel since high school when *The Clan of the Cave Bear* movie came on cable TV one night while I was babysitting for the family down the street. (22, 23) The main character, Ayla, had courage and ingenuity and she did so many amazing things on her adventures. Throughout all the books though, her journey was always about finding a place where she would fit in, a place that she could call home. I always connected with her character, and like me, she never wanted to just pick just one thing. Ayla didn't see why you couldn't be a mother and a medicine woman and a hunter and be skilled at many different things. Her character represents the original feminist and a prehistoric entrepreneur. But it can be lonely to never quite belong anywhere. Since first reading those books I knew there was something in them that called to me, and being in the woods dancing around the fire to the beat of the drums connected me in a deeper way to that ancestral pull and helped me to tune in to parts of myself that had been lying dormant for too long.

Sometimes, when we don't create enough space in our lives to let the entirety of the sadness sink in, life sends us a moment that is so powerful that it brings the memories close enough to feel them again whether we think we are ready or not. Even giving myself time to go on retreat and join in the grief ritual had not released all of the sadness from the depths of my heart. I had been moving through this season of grieving and loss, but as the mother, there were so many counting on me and I had to be strong for them. In the autumn of that same year, it was clear that it was time for my beloved cat to transition from this life, and I felt very strongly that I wanted to be alone with him and hold space for his passing. He was my first pet, and I had brought him home when he was a kitten. He had always slept on my chest and I was worried what we would do when I brought home the babies. I have a picture of me nursing the twins with him lying right in between the two of them. He was not as helpful at my water birth, but he was always there by my side. I didn't know what I would do without him. I was glad that everyone else was in school so that I could hold him quietly and just take care of him, and not worry about holding space for everyone else's feelings at the same time. As I held my cat in my arms as he took his last breath and then exhaled into complete stillness, I felt like I was able to finally let my heart break open and all of the sadness that I had been holding came pouring out. In that moment, I was tuning in to the universal feeling of loss and letting go. I was feeling the immensity of the grief that comes when you hold someone that you love in your arms as they leave this world. I went out to the backyard and I dug a hole under his favorite tree. As I wrapped him in a beautiful blanket, I was sending my love to everyone who has had to do this with their baby or their beloved or their mother. As I lowered him down into the ground, I felt like I was leaving those pieces of my heart deep in the Earth. I still don't know how we are supposed to have the strength for moments like this, but I was starting to tune in to this inner knowing that it was not a part of the Mother's plan for us to do this alone.

I felt blessed that this women's retreat had connected me with so many people who had the answers that I had been seeking whether or not I could articulate the questions. (The word *Antevasin* means the spiritual seeker living on the edge, in the world but not of the world.) (24) I met the women who were instrumental in launching the Red Tent Temple Movement that was a grassroots community movement starting to make its way across the country. (25) Since the book *The Red Tent* by Anita Diamant had been published and translated into many languages and spread around the world, it had reawakened something in women that they hadn't even known was missing. The chain of grandmothers and mothers passing down their wisdom to the daughters had been broken so many generations ago that we didn't even know what we didn't know. Attempting to cleanse the Earth of its wise women during the burning times left the women that followed afraid to speak and afraid to stand out. So for generations afterwards, women were afraid to even wonder what was missing, but there was a secret longing just the same. Now the stories were starting to bubble up to the surface and the secrets were coming out into the light.

The next year, on Mother's Day, I started the Red

Tent Women's Circle in my community. It was based
on the list that I had made years before (which I still
have in our group's bin of supplies) and was created
specifically to be accessible and approachable for the
women in my area. Each month, I create a safe place
for us to gather and practice letting go of some of the
acculturated habits that no longer serve us, things
that we have learned since we were little girls just by
watching the women around us, like apologizing all
the time. I'm not referring to true remorse for when
we've done something wrong, but to that habit of being
sorry for existing, for taking up space, for daring to
have thoughts and feelings. In the red tent, we create a
woman space where we can practice letting go of those
things that we've been trained to think we are *supposed*
to do. When we do that, we can make room for the
things that will really allow us to live fully in alignment
with our passions and purpose and to have true joy
instead of grinning through the pain and saying that
it is "fine." The rest of the month we live our everyday
lives, follow our routines, do our work, and take care
of everyone else. And then for one evening each month
we create a cozy, safe, womanly, comfortable, and
nurturing space in which we can practice unfolding
our wings.

In the book *The Red Tent*, the author reminds us of a time when women would take a full three days off each month to sit with the women of the tribe (their grandmothers and mothers and aunts and sisters and cousins and daughters) and replenish their energy and share their wisdom. (26) They would pass down the ancient stories and songs and rituals. They would also dream together and receive powerful visions that would secure the health and safety of the tribe. In the Red Tent, they also had a safe and comfortable place for the women to give birth. And even the new mothers knew what to do because they had seen their mother and their aunt and maybe their sister give birth before it was their own birthing time. Even as recently as the last couple centuries, the settlers in the United States built their houses with a Borning Room off of the kitchen where all of the births and illnesses and deaths could be attended to by the family. (27) In the Red Tent, just like in those farmhouses on the prairie, the women gave birth surrounded by a group of women that they knew and trusted. They were not meant to do things alone like in modern times when our homes are spread far apart and we are expected to cook and clean and give birth and raise our children isolated and alone.

Over time, and in many cultures around the world,

they started to speak of the women's time away as a way for them to be banished while they were cursed with their monthly flow. Reading this book was so empowering because it made me realize that the women in this story were not banished; they were released from their regular, mundane duties to attend to the sacred. They were not dirty or cursed, they were powerful. In some religions and cultures today, you will still hear the men speak with a knowing that they need to stay away from the women during that time of the month because they are more open to the Divine, and they are even more powerful at that time. In cultures that are balanced and healthy, the men honor and protect the women so that they can do their important work of going within and connecting to the wisdom of the universe and of their ancestors. They know that this work is essential to the survival of us all.

I created my women's circle because I had wanted the women in my community to be able to come together in a more authentic way, even if it was just for one night that we carved out of the rest of the month while we are busy maintaining our modern lifestyle. I had been searching for something like this for a while and I was happy to find a movement that gave it a name. There were social media pages and a map of available locations so that women who were interested in this type of thing could find us. (28) Dr. Isadora Leidenfrost had made a movie called "The Things We Don't Talk About" (which featured a lot of the women that I had met on retreat) and we held a screening event with a panel discussion at my local library. (29) It was funny that I ended up being the one who was called to start this group, because a part of me was still that little girl who was afraid to wear red because it attracted too much attention (maybe it was my puritan ancestors who were rolling over in their graves at the thought of that scarlet letter or maybe it was because of my wounds in that base chakra) and it felt too dangerous. Years ago at my cousin's wedding reception, a lovely woman had leaned over while we were sitting at the table eating our dinner and she told me that I should wear red because it would be perfect with my coloring, but I had never gotten up the courage. I wanted this women's circle to exist and I wasn't going to wait any longer for someone else to start it, so I pushed past the fear and I made it happen. I was able to create a feeling of "safe space" because we gathered in small groups in private spaces and only women who were really searching would find us. But now that we were trying to reach out to more women and let them know that this kind of thing is available and why it is so important, I had to go public. I was asked to sit up front and speak at the movie screening, and then they asked me to write about our Red Tent for the holistic health column in the newspaper.

Speaking your truth and having the wounds in your lower chakras witnessed brings the secrets into the light. This not only dissolves the blockages and allows those lower energy centers to heal, the act of expressing yourself is also tremendously healing for your 5th chakra. If those truths remain unspoken, the stories stay locked up in our cells and are unavailable for healing. (30) In the Red Tent we have a sacred, confidential healing circle that holds space for you to gently release the stories that have been a burden for too long. Even if you are not ready to speak, you can be part of the circle and bear witness to others as they come out of their cocoon and you can continue to gather strength from their example until you are ready. For some women, just letting the others look at them and send them love while they silently hold the talking stick (or beads or bowl) is an important practice in receiving. And when they are ready to let their cocoon fall away, when the bud gently starts to open, they have a circle of women to hold space for them and to celebrate with them. Many times we just need to speak to the fact that this feels scary, or uncomfortable, or weird. We've seen in the news that we need more hugs. We know that we crave that healthy nurturing touch that comes with no strings attached. But some of us don't know how to ask for it. Maybe we need people who understand that sometimes we are freaking out inside, but we are pushing past that feeling because we want it to be easier for the next generations. We have lost much of our link to the old women's traditions and we may not know how our ancestors actually did this, but we can create our own ceremonies (with rituals as simple as lighting a candle and setting aside some time) that work for us, and that in its own way is powerful.

For those of you who have been told that your forms of expression are improper or that you are too old now (or whatever limiting belief is holding you back), the red tent creates a safe place for you to get your creative juices flowing. You can do art projects (scribble, color, paint, knit, make a mandala, or create a Zentangle®) as a form of mindfulness meditation. I started using the Zentangle® method a few years ago, and it is a perfect practice for me because there is no right way to do it. (31)You can't make a plan. You have to just see what comes from adding one stroke of your pen at a time until a work of art emerges. You use permanent ink, so there is no changing your mind; you need to just accept what is. You make the tangle, like a loop of rope, and then fill each section with a different pattern. For people who are usually too busy answering to the clock and the calendar and the spreadsheet, a simple art project can connect you to the creative side of your brain again. You don't have to show anyone your projects; it is just the art of letting your creativity flow that is restorative. I have shared some of my drawings with you in this book. I made one pen-drawing for each of the chapters. The patterns that I used to fill in my trees and butterflies are from the Zentangle® method. Later on in this book, you will see how I took the drawing from my blessing way (that I shared in my first book) with the young mother cradling the spiral of her belly and elevated her expression with a patterned mandala Zentangle®.

Just knowing that the Red Tent will be here in just a few short weeks lets me promise my body that I will come back to any feelings that came up when I didn't have time to fully process them. If I know that I will give myself time to really feel them soon, then they don't need to keep nagging at me. Sometimes we are in the middle of some other obligation and we have somewhere to be. Sometimes we need to hold it together because we are at work, or have to keep functioning because we are the one who takes care of everyone else. So we tuck the grief or the anger or the joy away where it can't slow us down. I wish that we had three days every month, but I will take my three hours and make it count for now. (Trying to finish all the grocery shopping and get back in time for preschool pick-up has taught me to be quite efficient with my time.) Sadly, I've found that many women will not even give themselves permission to ask for three hours off each month to do something for their own self-care. I totally understand because I've been there myself, but I want to tell them that it doesn't make sense, because if they came they would feel better and be even more efficient and effective the rest of the month. When I'm sitting alone in my suburban home, folding laundry fresh from the dryer, sometimes I long for the sisterhood that women had when they all went to the river to wash the clothes together. Now I understand why my grandmother would have the soap opera playing on her TV in the background everyday while she completed the household chores alone and isolated out in her little house in the woods.

Your emotions can be like toddlers that are trying to get your attention. First they call to you nicely in their sweet little voice. Then they go on repeat: "Mommy,

Mommy, Mommy…" Then they fling themselves into a full thrashing and screaming tantrum. If we give voice to our emotions when they ask nicely, they will feel acknowledged and will be satisfied. If we stuff them down or hide them away, they show up as physical symptoms and get bigger and louder and more annoying until you have to stop everything else and deal with the pain. If we are less distracted and start to react more quickly and notice the feelings (or our actual toddlers) right away, we can stop the progression.

Now when I first have an inkling of a tickle in my throat, I gargle with essential oils, drink extra fluids, and get some extra rest so that I'm not sick in bed for days with a sore throat and a fever. After I had a really bad breast infection when the twins were newborns, I was on hyper-alert for the signs and symptoms and would fly into action at the first painful twinge with extra rest, heat packs and baby-snuggles with extra nursing to avoid ever experiencing that again. And if the school nurse sends home a note that says lice is going around school, then I get out the tea-tree oil and special shampoo and I go on the offensive before they can even think about bringing that home to my house! Yes, again, I learned the hard way. I seriously had no idea how tiny those things are and I totally missed it the first time I tried to check my own kids' heads. If you miss just a few tiny eggs, they can hatch and take over your world. It is so much work to get rid of them once they have settled in to every nook and cranny of your home. The very day that I had folded and organized all of the piles of summer clothes to bring up to the attic and had also brought down all of the winter clothes to inventory, was when the note came home from school saying to wash all of the clothes (and vacuum every rug, piece of upholstery, and curtains)! Whatever it is that needs our attention, we need to be responsive and proactive to notice those early warnings. If we can reconnect to our intuition on all fronts and learn to trust the messages that we receive, then we can avoid the bigger disasters or the more painful symptoms and then we won't feel like we're always in emergency mode trying to play catch up.

So in our world that runs by the clocks and the calendars, where we schedule and time-block everything, I choose to set aside an evening every month to sit with my true feelings. And it actually does work to promise your body that you will come back to it and really give it full expression, but only if your body learns to trust that you will keep that promise. You need to give yourself the time to own your feelings. Much of the time we are worried about everyone else. Maybe their grief is bigger, but we need to acknowledge where we are grieving too. Maybe your friend just lost their spouse, so you feel like you can't grieve losing your friend. Maybe someone else just lost their job, so you don't feel like you can complain that your dream job is not at all what you expected. In the Red Tent, we know that everyone's individual experience and perspective is valid, and we will hold space for whatever you are grieving. Similarly, we create space for bragging and for celebrating. We celebrate the little things as well as marking our rites of passage. Many women have been told that it is not lady-like to brag about their accomplishments so we give the credit away and downplay our contributions. In the Red Tent, we give ourselves permission to own the fullness of our creative powers.

When Grandma reached about 80 years old, she started expressing herself with much more honesty because she was starting to forget what was considered proper. She was freed from the social conditioning and she forgot what she was supposed to say. She would get so frustrated about forgetting things, but I found that there were now new stories surfacing that had been hiding behind the ones that she had already told *the reality of getting stuck in the story!*

me a <u>hundred times.</u> She had always been so strong and capable and it was hard for her to accept that she now needed some help. I took her home to my house to live with us for a while and it was really no trouble at all to set one more place at our family table. I was already accustomed to moving more slowly since I'd entered the phase of pushing baby strollers and following toddlers with short legs who *need* to walk by themselves, so <u>walking slowly with her fit into our rhythm just fine,</u> but she <u>always apologized</u> anyway. I got a folding stool that I'd use to help her in and out of the mini-van. I always felt awkward letting her push the stroller or the grocery cart, but it helped with her <u>balance</u> and it also <u>helped her feel like she was contributing.</u> I took her to all the community activities and school events and we'd find her a place of honor where she could watch the kids' performances or even to just sit and enjoy seeing them play at the park.

When she had been living alone in her house, she would easily forget what day it was since she had nowhere to be and she had no obligations. She would forget what time it was too, and might end up sleeping all day and getting up to eat a meal in the middle of the night. Being back in the rhythm of family life, with set meal times and people to talk to and activities on

longstanding tribal tradition of
old + young together

certain days of the week, she started to feel more in touch with reality and she started to remember things again. We would play games together and when the little ones would be learning their words, she was trying to remember them again. The 3-year-old and the 83-year-old could share in their frustration that the card with the green frog looked too similar to the one with the green turtle. Then they would start laughing and just eat the cereal pieces that they were using as their BINGO markers. After only a week of having a routine and people to keep her company, she started feeling smarter and more confident and she felt physically stronger and more coordinated.

I wanted her to stay at our house and I enjoyed that she was telling me more family stories than she ever had before, but she had a really hard time with letting me be the caretaker. She had always been the adult and I was the child. I hear parents talk about how little children have a hard time with transitions and we should give them presets like: "You can play for a few more minutes and then we're going to put on your shoes and go in the car." But even for those small transitions, the presets never work. We always want to play just a little bit longer. We don't like change. I came up with a new plan for those playground presets with my kids and I would just surprise them at the bottom of the slide and scoop them up and spin them around and then they'd be buckled into the stroller before they knew what happened. Then I could gently console them about the loss of their playtime as we walked to the parking lot. (But as you may know, when you have multiple children, you are lucky if the first kid is still in their shoes or jacket or stroller buckles or whatever by the time you get around to the last kid.) Anyway, even with all the cultural expressions and presets and warnings about getting older, it was harder for me to help Grandma move through this transition while she mourned the loss of her independence than it was to get 4 kids off of the playground at the same time.

Grandma insisted on going home to her own house, and I couldn't stop her. She had somebody to come and take her shopping once a week, but I didn't feel like it was enough. I wished that she lived closer. Her gardens kept her occupied, but when winter came she was stuck indoors all day, and I convinced her to visit with us again. This time was much harder. The last time that she had visited I had been able to leave her reading a book and napping while I went to meet a client for an appointment or drive the kids to something, but now I didn't feel like I could leave her alone. One time when I came back from the office I smelled burning and found bits of bread stuck to the burners on my electric stove. She had wanted to save electricity by not turning on the toaster. It's not like she didn't know her way around the kitchen. She was the best cook in the whole world. I'm serious. She lived in a town where the rich and famous people vacationed in the summers and they would all rather visit and eat at her small kitchen table than go to the fancy restaurants. Either way, I stayed home with her because I didn't feel safe leaving her alone anymore.

I fell behind on my work because we would have fun scavenger hunts looking for missing hearing aids or tiny pills or other time-consuming adventures, and I told my parents that I would love to stay home with her but maybe they could pay me what they would spend to hire a home health aide, and then I wouldn't have to worry about my lost income. My mom told me to just go to work and not worry about Grandma. I worried anyway. Then one morning Grandma went catatonic while I was getting the kids ready for the school bus. She was talking to me while I made sandwiches and then she just froze where she stood and started shaking and I called to my son to hold her so she wouldn't fall while I ran to get a chair. I called the ambulance and then the EMTs stayed with her while I took the kids out to the bus stop. When in doubt, you just keep going through the motions of your routine. Later, I called the school and had the counselor check on my kids (especially my son who had been the one to hold her) so she could help them process their own emotions about our crazy morning.

The EMTs said that Grandma had probably had a few minor strokes like this when she was at home alone. When a tree falls in the woods and nobody hears it, does it make a sound? Now I really felt out of my league and called my mother crying. She said that it was fine. My grandmother was the strongest person that I've ever known, but I was starting to learn that she was strong because she had always had to be. She clenched her fists so tightly against the world that she had been knotted up with arthritis since she was a young adult. Even when she was a young mother at home with little children to care for, she sometimes had to have my grandfather carry her because she was in too much pain to walk. She said that she was actually able to move better in her eighties because the medications had gotten so much better by that time. But all that stubborn clenching and resentment had grown into an inoperable tumor instead. Since there was nothing that the doctor could do, they said not to tell her about the tumor. But when she asked me why it hurt there, I would tell her. She was already frustrated that she couldn't remember things, so just for a moment it eased her mind for the pain to at least make sense.

All of those symptoms pointed to first chakra wounds, but nobody ever talked about what had happened. She never told me her stories until she started to forget what was supposed to be kept secret. It didn't really surprise me because I'd already had a glimpse of it from the repressed memories that had surfaced in my dreams after my VBAC. During that really difficult postpartum period it had taken me awhile to make sense of everything that was surfacing. I had to figure out where the memories had come from since they were not my own. First I had to realize that they were in fact, memories, since they were not from my lifetime. When she told me her stories, it confirmed what I had already suspected. Going through that experience is how I learned firsthand that if you leave your trauma unhealed and stuff the memories of it away, they can resurface later in unexpected ways. Part of me was a little egg inside of my mom when she was growing in my grandmother's womb. In addition to keeping my pantry stocked like we are still in the

Great Depression, I can also access my grandmother's memories in those moments when I go beyond the veil (like during transition in childbirth) or when the physical therapist releases the energy of those wounds from my fascia. After Grandma died, I received even more confirmation that those stories were true.

She hadn't wanted to stay in my house anymore. She had started getting aggressive because she thought that we were forcing her to stay when she wanted to go. She wanted to be home in the house that she had built with her own two hands alongside her husband so many years ago and she felt like we were keeping her away. She thought someone had taken her house. She couldn't relax. It finally overwhelmed her and she collapsed. As I sat on the floor holding my grandmother's head in my hands, the memory of my cat dying in my arms came back to me so intensely. Grandma had always been so strong, and now looking at her from above, so vulnerable and so small, was such an overwhelmingly touching moment. She was telling me that she couldn't die because everyone would be mad at her. She had too much that she still needed to do. But she was so tired. I stroked her hair and told her that she could rest now.

Back home in her own house, my cousin found her

lying on the kitchen floor one morning. She'd had an even bigger stroke and they didn't really know how long she'd been lying there before he found her. There was nothing they could do. She later died at home in her marriage bed, where my grandfather had died a few years earlier. At last, they could be together again. I wrote her a poem about being able to dance again. At her funeral, I read that poem and I sang her a song about being set free from her chains. What was left of the older generation of relatives were there and I heard even more stories and connected more dots. People would tell me things, but then say that it was a secret and I couldn't tell anyone else. I am the keeper of the secrets.

When I got home from that final trip to the house where I had spent my childhood holidays and vacations, the dreams started. I would wake up with a story that I knew was true, and I'd ask my relatives a question about a random detail or date to see if I could confirm the story without telling them what I was doing. Grandma told me more after she passed away then she had allowed herself to share when she was still here. She had really been set free. But now, what do I do with this information?

It's times like this that we really need something in

our life like what I had created in my Red Tent. Back in the day, they had quilting circles or the women would gather at the hair salon, but many of our communities are larger now, and there doesn't seem to be a place for women to express themselves. When we were first told the details about the funeral I got busy packing the suitcases and preparing to be out of town, and printing up the papers for the ceremony. I was functioning. I was strong. After traveling and getting settled, I got the kids dressed and into their fancy shoes and we met everyone at the cemetery. Someone actually mentioned that my baby was always so clingy, but they had only ever seen us at funerals! I'm okay with letting my kids feel sad when someone they love dies. I had to hold it together when I sang so that my voice would actually come out and not just get lost in the tears, but my husband helped me finish the song when I choked up and luckily it came out kind of like we had planned a duet. And then I picked up the shovel and started digging. They came and told me that someone else would do that, but I just kept digging. I needed to help create space for her to finally be held by the Earth Mother.

I promised myself that I would let myself feel everything soon in the safety of the Red Tent, and then

I was really able to take time to let myself grieve. For me to be able to take care of everyone else, I need a safe place where I can let other people take care of me. I help my kids learn to process their own feelings, and then I have others who do that for me. I'm from a culture that doesn't really talk about feelings, so my parents didn't have someone to model that for them when they were small, so they didn't know how to do that for me. I am trying to break that cycle for my kids, but it doesn't come naturally. I am hoping that if I learn to move with the cycles and the phases of my life that it will help me to be able to transition gracefully into old age when it is my children's turn to pack the car and make the sandwiches, and maybe I'll even be able to enjoy being waited on.

If I can learn from the stories and break the hold that these secrets have on my family, then maybe we won't be in so much pain anymore. Maybe if we don't hate our bodies, then they won't be inflamed with autoimmune diseases. As we bring our secrets out into the light and fully express our truth, and have our stories witnessed, they lose their power over us. If I teach my children to find safe ways to express themselves, and let them know that they can tell me anything, then they won't need to hide it away and make themselves sick with guilt and shame. And when they tell me about their dreams and the things that they just know to be true, I affirm them and acknowledge their power in the hopes that it will be easier for them in the long run if they keep their intuition intact in the first place instead of trying to piece it back together afterwards.

When I was three years old, I was awakened from my nap by a message that there was a monster coming to blow my house down. I went down the stairs to wake up my mother and I told her that we had to get out of the house because the monster was coming. She didn't believe me. She didn't trust me. I started to doubt my intuition. When the tornado came moments later, we didn't have time to get down to the basement, so she just pulled the afghan blanket over us and that protected us from the first blast of glass shards as the windows blew in. Another night, after we had rebuilt our home and we didn't have to sleep in the neighbor's living room anymore, I woke up screaming because I saw a monster standing outside my door watching me sleep. I was even more scared when the monster came closer to me despite my screams. It turned out that it was just my dad on his way to the bathroom and he had come in to my room to console me because I was so scared. But I can still feel how strong my initial reaction was in that moment. Another memory that stayed with me is of a day when my dad and I were walking hand-in-hand in the hardware store and he wanted to go one way, but I saw someone scary in that next room and I refused to go with him. He was holding my hand and pulled for me to follow, but I sat down with a determination so strong that I dislocated my elbow. He hadn't believed me that it was dangerous to go there. I wasn't scared of my dad, but I knew in my bones that those moments were scary, despite the adults telling me that everything was fine. For years I doubted my intuition, but then as I started to tune in to the truth of the old stories that were buried in secrecy for generations, I knew that I had been right all along and the image of a man standing in the doorway was burned into my cellular memory as a sign of danger. Tuning in to these memories from my childhood and realizing that I had always had the power to feel that truth in my bones helped me to start to trust my intuition, my dreams, and my visions again. I started to look for more ways to use my natural gifts.

As we start to awaken to our full nature, we need to be gentle with ourselves. A flower needs to blossom in its own time, we cannot pry the bud open with inpatient fingers and force it to unfurl its petals. If we did so we would ruin the blossom. Babies need to be given the opportunity to choose the timing of their own birth when they feel safe and ready to transition from one phase and commence with the next part of their journey. Unless it is a true emergency, babies need to be allowed to complete those final stages of development that happen with the caress of the contracting uterus as their mother labors. A butterfly needs to come out of its cocoon at just the right moment, with the precise temperature and sunlight that will support its final transformation. When my kids studied butterflies in school, I was amazed at how complex the whole process is. We probably studied this when I was in elementary school too, but I feel like I am learning much more the second time through. When the butterfly emerges, it needs to hang upside down and let the blood flow to the wings as they spread out and dry. If it doesn't have time to fully spread its wings before they dry out, then they will remain stunted and it will not be able to fly. So even if you have dreams of flying and achieving great heights, it is vital that you give yourself time to spread your wings and develop your skills first. Even butterflies need to learn to stand before they can take flight.

Things to think about:

- Which stories need to be told? What truths do you need to speak? Pay attention to when you hold yourself back or swallow your words.

- What are some symptoms that you have gotten used to living with? Are they keeping you from living your life? Remember back to the first time you felt that symptom. How old were you then? Do you remember what else was going in your life at that time? Has it gotten worse over time?

- What types of art projects did you like when you were a kid? Did you like to dance or sing? How long has it been since you have created something? How can you start to express yourself more completely?

- Art therapy is a great way to get out of your head and into your body. Try creating a Zentangle® or make a mandala. Knit something. Get your hands in some play-dough or make some bread. What else could you try?

- What types of ceremonies can you create to celebrate your accomplishments or to fully express your grief? You can gather with others or find a quiet place to carve out a few hours for yourself.

Chapter 6: Holding Space for the Vision

The 6th chakra is thought of as the third-eye and it includes the brain, eyes, and nose, but it especially pertains to the pituitary and pineal glands. The way that I have learned to understand it is that this is where we pick up messages from the universe or the collective consciousness, like when we pray for someone because they suddenly come to mind. The power of our thoughts can impact the rest of our health, so it is good to keep those good vibrations going. The importance of mental health has become even more evident in recent years, but it's no surprise that an optimistic attitude can make any situation seem better. They say that we not only need to learn to see the glass as half full, we need to see it as refillable. We also need to make sure that we are focused on the glasses that we are personally responsible for, and not try to fill every glass in the world. Just like we spread ourselves too thin emotionally when we are trying to take care of everyone else, we also use too much mental energy worrying about things that haven't happened yet and we become fearful and anxious about things that are out of our control.

When children reach 5 years old, they are coming into their full selves, and tuning in to their vision of who they want to be when they grow up. This is also a huge year for them mentally as they start to measure their world in hours and minutes. They also may start learning how to read words and write sentences, and with this, they start telling stories more chronologically as they learn to order their thoughts in that way. I think this new way of seeing the world also changes the way in which children store their memories, more logically and systematically, and less emotionally. It is fun to help them learn all of these new skills, but it's also a good time to teach them to handle frustration if something doesn't come easily. Show them how to learn from their failures, and then try again. They can learn to enjoy new things, instead of backing down from the challenge. A good toolkit of mental health strategies will help them when they face their next phases of existential crisis at 12 and 19 years old.

Of course, the more you are able to calm yourself down, stay cool under pressure, and think clearly, the more that you will be able to model that for your kids. If you are in survival mode, using all of your energy to worry about how you are going to pay the bills, or how to keep yourself safe, then you will not have any energy for learning. When you are stuck in the fight/flight/freeze response, the reasoning part of your brain actually shuts down. This is why the effects of abuse, trauma, and chronic stress show up so clearly in the classroom. Even if you have no recollection of anything traumatic happening in your family history, there may be stories that you don't remember, or that were passed down from previous generations. If your biochemistry was wired for a stressful or dangerous environment, it often shows up as anxiety, depression, or learning disabilities. If you have a block or imbalance in this energy center, sometimes you experience it as a fear of self-evaluation, a fear of being open to the ideas of others or even paranoia. (30) Reflecting on your life experiences, learning from your mistakes, looking at the big picture, and thinking outside the box are good ways to start to shift your mental energy back towards healthier thought patterns.

While deep reflection and expressing your truth are important, you need to make sure that you aren't skipping over the often overlooked planning phase. While every action needs to take place in the present moment, you need to occasionally stop being busy with the life that you've already created long enough to reconnect with your vision for the future. The sixth energy center is all about knowledge and introspection and focusing on your personal vision. The first step in creating your vision is to reconnect with your true self. When you first start practicing to speak your truth, you may hear something come out of your mouth that sounds like someone else. Listen to those expressions and think of where they came from; maybe they are the voice of a parent, friend, teacher or society in general. When you speak it out loud, you gain clarity as it becomes more obvious. When you start to tune back in to your own intuition and embrace the way that you truly feel, you start to be able to separate out those feelings that you thought you were supposed to have or things that you should do or that you are meant to believe. When you bring these beliefs out into the light, you can turn them around and look at them from different angles and see if they still feel true. And then you can choose whether to keep them or to replace them with a new belief that feels more in alignment with your vision.

You can start by reflecting on how you've felt in each of your activities, projects, jobs, and relationships to begin to tune in to what really makes your heart sing. Even in the jobs that you ended up hating, think of what attracted you to that position in the first place. Maybe you liked the job in the beginning, but then either the job changed, or you changed. Maybe you just liked the description of the job, but then the reality did not match. Think of the parts that you did enjoy. In those tough relationships, think of what it was that you were seeking and how maybe reality fell short of your expectations, but what you desired in the first place was valid. Then you can consciously choose which aspects of that vision to nourish and encourage and which things you can put aside, compost, or delegate to someone else.

◆

Before I could even think about letting good things into my life, I needed to stop pushing them away. The first step was to bring more awareness to when I was doing it. One way (especially as women) in which we express this scarcity mindset is in thinking that if we have something nice then it means that we are taking it away from someone else. So I wouldn't accept it when something good came along, because surely someone else deserves good things more than I do. Even when it is something as simple as when someone paid me a compliment, I would feel that I needed to push it away, deny it, or explain it away instead of just receiving it. If someone said that my dress was pretty, I would say "oh, this old thing?" or "I found a great sale," or I'd go with the full denial and say "oh, no, I'm such a mess" or "I was afraid it made me look fat." So, before I could even start to accept the fact that they were trying to be nice or trying to connect with me, or maybe even allow myself to think that they were really saying that not only the dress was nice, but that I looked pretty in it, I needed to stop instinctively pushing away the compliment. So I practiced just saying "Thank you" and smiling. It was really hard work.

Breaking a habit (something that we were raised to do, trained ourselves to do, or something that everyone has done for so long that we don't even know we do it) takes time. In the same season that I was rehearsing for Godspell, I took a training program for creating success in your business. In the first workshop, they told us that it takes 21 days to make a new habit. The first few times that you try the new action (when you hear the compliment: stop, take a breath, don't push it away, say "thank you", and smile) it takes an incredible amount of conscious effort. If you can push through until you've actually done it 21 times in a row, then you'll find that now you can do it more naturally.

We formed smaller accountability groups and we met for 8 weeks during the course of the success training, because most people need to start over about 7 times. For example, if you are practicing receiving compliments and you argue and say "oh, this old thing" or a similar dismissal, then you have to go back to the beginning of the 21 day challenge. It's like those factory posters that say "12 days without an injury" and sometimes the number gets really high and then they have one accident on the job and have to reset it to zero. The early weeks of the program were spent identifying what habits and self-limiting beliefs were keeping you from succeeding in reaching your goals. Then you needed to visualize what you could try instead. It helped to have other people give feedback, and help you to find perspective. Even after identifying what you want to change, it's not easy to change those core beliefs. It is good to practice with something small. Even with a new habit that seems easy to adopt, you might need a few tries to get it right. So, by the 7th or 8th time we met, maybe everyone had had a chance to decide on one new behavior that they could implement, and some were on their way to doing it 21 times in a row. Some take the program again and again because it is so eye-opening, but it takes many attempts to get started. Many people drop out of the program because it pushes them too far outside of their comfort zone.

It actually ended up being perfect timing that I was taking the business success program at the same time that I was rehearsing for Godspell because the "deepest fear" quote that I had to read in the opening scene went really well with what I was learning to put into practice in my life and my business. (20) Sitting in that room full of professionals, I realized that our deepest fear is not failure, it is success. We stick to what we know. We fear change. But I knew that if I could let myself heal and let people see my transformation, then it would help others to see how much they could change as well. In the workshops, we would create our own vision of success and then identify how you could use your business to help create the life that you want, instead of creating a life around your job. Some of the people showed us how to have a 4-day work week and some even designed a life that only required a 4-*hour* work week. They were focused and driven and accomplished all of their objectives efficiently and then could truly enjoy their time off knowing that the work was done and everything was in place for future growth.

We started the program by exploring the root cause of our fears and what stories we were telling ourselves about money and success. Many people (no matter how old) were still trying to make their parents proud, and some were doing work that they hated because it was what was expected of them. Many times we model our lives after someone else's success, and we think that if we follow their steps and copy their actions then we can achieve the same outcome. It never works because we need to follow our own path and define our own success. We each have our own purpose and we need to take steps on our own journey. It is so important to find good role models and mentors, but even the best teacher cannot do the work for us.

Many of these business programs are taught by men, so I needed to start by finding mentors and models of success that made more sense for my reality as a working mom. But I did learn a lot through that program and it was really interesting to learn that the top business professionals are using the Law of Attraction. (32) They believe in energy work, and practice things like visualizations and speaking your affirmations out loud to shift their mindsets. Using these strategies consistently creates a real framework for personal as well as financial and business success and it is not fringe or alternative after all. There are a number of articles about successful entrepreneurs (and in America that means that their companies made a lot of money) that seem to pinpoint what process they use and it turns out that they were the ones who learned to tune in to their intuition and trust their gut reactions. (33) The big stories are about the ones who are really good at reading people and acting on their instincts. When I read these business articles it sounds like being an empath with high self-esteem combined with vision, purpose, and the right timing is the recipe for success.

But, despite all of this research that supports what some call "soft skills," many of the business training programs are formulated from a very masculine perspective. My teacher was great, but the strategies employed by a confident and energetic, single young man with all the time in the world and no family obligations were not easily applicable to my current reality. So in addition to these workshops, I found role models in books written by moms who also ran businesses. And then I could apply the tools that they taught in the class like time-blocking and use them to block out all of my family activities first, and then fit my clients in second. I was happy that I could put "Kindergarten story time" and "Little League" and "church" and "family dinner" as the priorities. Then in between those, I would block out time to do my work. And then I could fit in other things like grocery shopping and cleaning the house with some flexibility. When I scheduled appointments, I could map out which errands I could stop and do on the way there or on the way home to be more efficient with my gas, but even more importantly, my time.

I also mapped out the life that I wanted and I learned to fit in all of the most important things each day. I learned to multitask and sing while I washed the dishes and pray over the kids' sandwiches before I put them in their lunchboxes (infusing the simple food with powerful intentions) and have meaningful conversations with the kids while driving in the minivan between activities. Just when I was becoming a super multi-tasking marvel, articles started coming out saying that it was not possible to multitask. But those articles were not written by moms. You probably have your own list of priorities, but for me some of the big things on my list of what I need to do daily include hugs, prayers, reading and singing. Then there are more things that I try to balance out over the week. I like to make my family home-cooked meals for most of our dinners each week. I like to spend time in nature. And although I don't list cleaning my house or doing laundry as my dream activities, I like to have a house that is clean enough that I'm not totally embarrassed if a friend stops by and I like to have clean clothes that are folded and sorted so that they are easy enough to find when I'm trying to get everyone out the door in the morning. When we are time-blocking our activities, that tells us *where* we need to be and when, but this list of values helps us to focus on *how* we will be and *why*.

One way that I can use my time efficiently is by taking two of the important things on my daily list and doing them at the same time. You can make your own list of priorities and try out different combinations, but one that I like is combining prayer and exercise. You can say your positive affirmations while you work out. You can say them out loud if you are bold, or in your head is fine, too. It might depend on whether you work out at home or at the gym. You can work out in the morning and visualize successful outcomes for each of the activities that you have planned for the day. You can send love to each part of your body while you stretch, because it makes your cells happy to be acknowledged, and then your body remembers to include them in metabolism instead of leaving forgotten pockets of fat somewhere. Another tool that helps with invigorating your skin and rejuvenating your detoxifying systems is to gently run a dry brush over your skin from your extremities towards your heart. When I was first learning this, I was again thankful that other women had made videos showing me how to get started until it became second nature. I started trying this before my shower in the morning, starting with brushing the bottoms of my feet and working up my legs, then brushing from my hands up to the tops of my arms. If you have trouble loving yourself, or being naked, when you are waiting for the water to warm up for your shower could be a good time to try this since you already have your clothes off and you are in a private place. Adding dry skin brushing to your self-care routine can give you a task to do that wakes up your cells while you also practice intentionally sending love to all of the parts of yourself.

One woman that I know that has easily and

confidently made millions of dollars told me that her secret to success is that she starts each day with saying a rosary. After I got back on my feet after my surgery, but still wasn't up to a full workout yet, I would roll out of bed in the morning (literally rolling to the side because it is easier on your abs than sitting straight up) and gently begin to stretch on the floor next to my bed, sometimes before I even opened my eyes. Then, I would greet the day and do some "sun salutation" yoga poses and say a decade of the rosary (one Our Father and ten Hail Mary's,) holding a different pose for each prayer. Whenever someone that I love dies, I usually go and find somewhere quiet to sit in nature, and I say a full rosary. I work my way around the rosary holding the beads between my fingers, and say all five repetitions of the decade of prayers. For a morning routine, saying one decade took me about twenty minutes. I've noticed that other cultures also use prayer beads and mantras that you repeat over and over during meditation. Some yoga classes start with a chant, and even business workshops start with speaking positive affirmations. Some successful people write their positive thoughts on post-its and stick them to their mirrors so that they remember to say them out loud before starting their day. You can try different ways to start your day with positive intentions for your body and your soul, and find whatever works for you, but I love coming up with my own combinations like my morning *"yogary."* Repeating affirmations, mantras, or prayers that you've known since childhood can interrupt your negative thought patterns and focus your energy in the present.

When I started feeling better, I began doing more of a full cardio workout in the morning with my husband, but I could still pray and visualize while I moved my body. We tried to get some workout videos that we liked and then repeat them. When your muscle memory is established, you don't need to pay attention with the same mental focus and your mind can go elsewhere. A lot of times, where my mind went was a way for me to make new habits about loving my body and my life. It still takes work, but maybe if I get to 21 days in a row it will get easier. They say, for mindfulness meditation, to be the observer and watch your thoughts. I'd hear myself think "wow, I can't believe I just jumped that high," and then, "I remember when it hurt to walk, this is awesome, this feels good, this is amazing." It can go all the way to, "If I can do this, I wonder what other new things I can try that I thought I'd never be able to do." These new thoughts are so much better than when I used to obsess about how ugly I was and how I would never be enough and about how my body hated me. So I honor how amazing it is to finally feel good in my body. Then for meditation, it is nice if you can get past the place of thinking into the place of just being, and find peace. Sometimes you'll be moving and working out and not thinking anything at all and not even noticing that you are moving because now you don't have to consciously will your legs to move, they just do, and then all of sudden the video ends and you don't know how you got there. That is how you find some time off from worry, from guilt and shame, and from regrets and analysis, and you are just present. It sneaks up on you. You find yourself in the moment.

Don't feel discouraged if you aren't there yet, because it is not easy and it can take a lot of practice. You have to choose to push past the part where your negative thoughts creep in and tell you that you are too tired and too sore and it's too hard and you'll never get there. Maybe you don't even try that jump for weeks and weeks, but then someday you try it and you're amazed to find that your feet left the floor. If you have stitches that pull when you move, please start with gentle stretching and stretch a little more each day and appreciate the progress. Someday you'll surprise yourself. We keep encountering these moments when it can become easier to quit. My husband and I used to work out in the evenings when he got home from work, but then we were getting to this phase where the kids were starting to have more things to do, like soccer games and school concerts and scout meetings, so we would have more and more evenings when we weren't even home. My chiropractor said that it was better to work out in the morning anyway, because it energizes you for the day, instead of keeping you from sleeping well at night. But we were already waking up at 6 a.m. on school days to get everyone out the door. It seemed crazy to think of getting up even earlier, but instead of arguing, I just set my alarm for 5:30 a.m. and kept at it until the new habit felt like an old routine. Exercising in the morning (and praying and checking in with each other) ended up being something nice that we could do together in the quiet moments before all the kids woke up.

The benefits of feeling better in your body and choosing the more positive thought start to spread to all the other parts of your life. I thought back to this one day when I was struggling through leading a Girl Scout activity for a bunch of little girls while wearing my abdominal brace and it was so hot outside and I was itchy and sweaty but I was trying to put on my happy face. When summer came around again the year after my surgery and I didn't have to wear that brace, I was so grateful. And it wasn't just the noticeable lack of pain and discomfort, it felt so good to be strong again. I had not fully realized how feeling so powerless in my body had been creeping into other aspects of my life. Feeling strong and able to run away from danger made me feel safer in my body, and it made me realize how unsafe I had been feeling, which had caused my whole body to be locked in trauma-mode. As I did my Mixed Martial Arts workout video and I kicked and punched the air (even though I'm against violence) it felt good to think that I may be able to stand up for myself or protect my kids, if needed. I realized how much of my parenting had been justifiably centered around being on guard to protect my kids from the dangers of the world. I would force myself to sit back and let my kids gain their confidence while climbing to the top of the playground. I was proud of myself for that because I saw that other moms were pulling their kids off of the equipment, or hovering and holding on, or not even bringing them to the park at all. So I let my children climb, but I was still on alert the whole time. Tuning in to my intuition and feeling confident in my physical strength felt good, but reconnecting to both aspects reminded me that I was still coming from that perspective of a victim. I was strong and I was a survivor, but I felt like I had to be strong because I was not safe. I wanted to get to where I really felt safe and at home in my body. I still had work to do.

I found an online group of moms that were healing after traumatic births. I was a few years out and I could be there to support the mothers who were suffering from the effects of fresh traumas while trying to care for their newborns and often other young children as well. I was also there for myself, too. Many of these women were also dealing with repressed memories that had surfaced, or found themselves re-traumatized, and in the moment that should have been beautiful and empowering, they found themselves victimized once again. These women were strong and they were amazing. They kept going and they fought for their kids, but this was another thing that they'd had to survive. Some days my memories or emotional wounds would surface again in unexpected ways and it was good to know where I could go and find other women who wouldn't tell me to just "get over it." Their stories encouraged me to keep doing the work and keep trying to break those old patterns that were not serving me. These women reinforced the idea that the work that I was doing to improve my own health and to create a better world for my kids could also be an example for other moms who wanted to heal but had no idea how to start.

Hearing stories from other women who had traumatic births helped me to focus on how important it is for us to heal our birth culture. If we can help these women to enter motherhood with confidence and physical and emotional health, then it will have a huge impact on the next generation. Even in a perfect system, with excellent providers, there are some really stressful moments during birth. Many women find that this is the hardest thing that they have ever done, physically and emotionally and spiritually. There is no changing your mind or having someone else do it for you. Sometimes there are unforeseen complications. What makes the birth traumatic is not just about what happened, but how the woman was treated and how she felt at the time. Feeling unheard, and feeling like you have no power or choice, is what leaves the biggest scar. If the mother feels like she can tune in to her inner knowing, then she will let you know when she needs support. If she understands why she needs an intervention and chooses to let the midwife or doctor help, then she can mentally process what is happening and emotionally heal afterwards, no matter how physically challenging it is. If she feels coerced or violated, then it will harder to heal from that same medical intervention. If you feel like your birth was traumatic, and you have not found someone who has held space for you so that you can speak your truth about your birth, reach out and find a support group either in your local community or online.

Being a part of these really personal discussions with these other mothers helped us all to feel less alone, but it made me even more convinced that doulas and midwives were the key to saving the world from the mess that we've made in the last few generations. If everyone had a great start to their life and had parents who felt supported and were equipped to fully nurture and love their babies in a safe home environment, then those babies would have their biochemical pathways wired for a long and healthy life instead of being calibrated for stress. I had already created a continuing education curriculum for a doula workshop and now I needed to find the courage to start putting myself out there and teaching it. When I was in my business success program, I realized how much I really needed to be doing this important work. I couldn't follow someone else's business plan, and I didn't need to be spending so much time doing work that someone else could do, I needed to be doing my life's work. I needed to create my own model. I needed to complete the assignment that the universe had given to me, because that was work that nobody else would do in the same way. I needed to teach again, and using what I had learned about business, I could find the people who wanted to learn what I had to teach. So I submitted my curriculum for my Birth Support for Survivors workshop and I had it approved for continuing education hours for doulas.

After stretching out her wings, the newly hatched butterfly needs to sit on the branch in the sunshine for a bit to rest and to gather her strength. She needs to tune in to her ancestral instincts while also calibrating to the current environment. She looks out beyond the horizon and she prepares for flight.

This phase of preparing to fly as you look towards manifesting your vision is often easier to think of with an airplane analogy since that is how more of us have actually experienced flight. As you sit in the plane and wait for take-off, the first thing that you feel is the cabin pressure increasing. As you force yourself to swallow to pop your ears, and you adjust your tray table and reach for your gum (and nurse your baby if you brought one,) you can tell that it is almost time. As if the cost of the ticket and the social pressure of everyone's expectations were not enough, then they lock those exterior doors and you know that you really can't change your mind now. There is no going back, you can't get out of this; you'll have to go through with it. As the plane starts to move, everything is rattling and vibrating and you are shaking and you know that you are getting close. And then, without even knowing how it is physically possible, you feel this huge, heavy, metal airplane lift off of the ground and float on the air. As it goes up and up into the sky, you see the buildings get smaller and smaller as your old life falls behind you, and then you remember to breathe as you break through the clouds and you now exist on an entirely different plane.

Our life goes through stages of change like this. I used to get so nervous when I felt the pressure increasing. It can be easier to go back to our comfort zone and stick to what we know. When we can endure the pressure and the shaking, we then push through to where things in our life start falling away. Maybe that old existence just doesn't fit anymore. Maybe those old shoes have suddenly gone from comfortable to worn out, and they aren't comfortable anymore. Your old life (like those shoes) is too small now, and is probably worn out and it is time for something shiny and new. But do you feel like breaking in a new pair of shoes? There is that period of time where they just seem too new. They don't feel like yours. You're not used to them. You miss your old shoes. You miss your old life where you knew what to expect, what to do and what to say. Everything moves in stages. Just as we get really good at something, we graduate. After a short celebration we find that we are back to being clueless freshman at the bottom of the next stage. So, when everything starts moving and shaking (maybe friends fall away and opportunities dry up) we need to put on our new shoes (with no pebbles in them) and look forward and know that we are ready to take flight and rise to the occasion.

When I first saw *The Birth of Magdalena* for sale online, I ran outside and I was gagging and heaving and sobbing in the yard. My conditioning around my fear of being seen was so strong that seeing my story in print made me physically sick. My first step was just to not take the site down. I fought through the same instinct when someone hung a flyer for my workshop in a public place. I had been marketing directly to doula groups and allowing them to see the real me, but having that flyer taped up on a wall in my hometown meant that anyone could see me. As I gather more evidence and my logical brain realizes that

I have indeed survived all of those exposures, maybe it will tell my emotional body that it is safe. Until then, I use a tool called Emotional Freedom Technique (EFT) or tapping which is a Do-It-Yourself emergency acupressure session that is free, readily accessible, and easy. There are videos online that you can use to practice at home until you get really good at it, and then you can do it while driving the minivan or walking through the grocery store or with your hands under the table during meetings. (34) There is also a book that you can use to teach your kids and it helps you to teach them how to calm down when something triggers them by physically tapping on these "magic spots" on your body. (35) In the moment when you are triggered by something that sets off a traumatic memory (even if you have no conscious memory of why it bothers you,) the negative emotions disrupt your energy. To quickly counteract this and to re-balance the body, you just tap on your energy meridian points with your fingertips and say positive things to yourself. (36) It works really well as a tool to calm down and restore your energy flow in the moment when something is being freshly triggered. There are also trauma healing practitioners that you can work with if you want to dive in and look more deeply at why it triggers you so that you can entirely remove the block from your system.

I started using EFT in the moment to bring my reactions down to a level that was more realistic for my current reality. When I was late to pick up my kid from preschool and I started thinking about all of the negative things (like that I was a bad mom and the other moms would judge me and my kid would feel abandoned), I could use EFT to start calming my body while I wired in some positive thoughts that are more realistic. Even good moms get stuck behind construction vehicles sometimes. The other moms have been there, too. My kid is not abandoned, he is safe with teachers that are really kind and know how to handle this. It is only 5 minutes, for *Pete's sake*. And I learned that they actually have a special job that the kids take turns helping with when they are the last one picked up, and they love it. So the next time this happens to you, while tapping on those magic spots, practice saying: "Even though I hate being late, I know that I am a good mom and I love and accept myself completely."

One day, I was on the way to teach a health class, and I started to get the sniffles. I immediately started to go down that road of negative self-talk thinking to myself that I was a fraud and wondering how could I teach about how to stay healthy if I had a cold. So I started tapping while I sat in my minivan at the red light and I accepted that even healthy people sometimes get a runny nose. Our body is wonderfully designed to fight off infection in that way. It means that my body is working. My students know that it is winter and probably won't think anything of it. And I could teach them about how when I first started to experience the signs that my body was fighting something off, I could support it with extra rest, fluids, nutrition, and some essential oils. I could share the process, and when I showed that I was a real person, I could connect with them in a more authentic way than when I was trying to always seem perfect. You can try tapping at home for lots of little things, like: "Even though I'm making cereal for dinner, all that matters is that we are together and we are fed." And then all that everyday practice will pay off when something really traumatic happens and you can use these tools for those big moments when you have to tell yourself that just because you lost your job or your best friend, it doesn't mean that your life is over, it is just time to move into another phase.

If you are not there yet, all of those positive sayings posted on walls and printed on t-shirts can be kind of annoying. When I first saw or heard comments from people that said, "Just think positive thoughts," I was like: "I don't get how you do that." But even while those people were a little too sickeningly sweet, I was kind of getting tired of being so bitter. It made me think and it made me start to look for opportunities to learn. There are steps to take to get there, and I needed to start at the beginning and be patient with myself as I moved towards the new way of being. First, I had to reframe the negative emotions to a more flat, neutral feeling. Then I could start shifting it to more positive thoughts. When your thought patterns and biochemistry have been wired for stress, and your mind and body have the habit of jumping straight into disaster mode, it takes time and effort to re-wire that. After learning more about energy healing, I found that the re-wiring can be done fairly quickly, but then you still need to go through the longer process of integrating the changes into your life, and forming new habits. And when you find that your mind and body have shifted into a new way of being, your life and your relationships need to stretch to accommodate the changes.

Practicing the EFT helped when I taught my first Birth Support for Survivors workshop for doulas and I shared my story, for the first time, out loud and face to face. It had taken a lot of courage to share it in the pages of my book, but this was live and they could look at me. I had been teaching for decades at this point, but never something so personal and so important. When the women went on their break, I sat there and centered myself and re-charged. When I read the evaluations at the end of the day, and learned that I had been able to really connect with these women, and that they were going to use what they had learned to help others, it was all worth the effort of pushing through that discomfort and into a new phase of growth.

Teaching about how to support victims of abuse and trauma can be triggering for the attendees, because even though they are professionals, they are still human. Women especially, tend to feel others pain when they tune in to the story. Oftentimes, people are drawn to the work of supporting others because they themselves have been there or know someone who has, so they come to the workshop not just for education, but because they are carrying their own stories that need healing. I set up my workshops to be an emotionally safe space for sharing. I pay a lot of attention to the physical space as well as the energetic feel of the room. You can be in a nicely decorated room, but if you keep hearing people walk by the door and the door might open at any time, then it doesn't feel safe and you will be more on guard and not able to really dive in to the material. The room needs to be physically comfortable and you need to feel like you have permission to move around as needed. Sometimes as we hear stories that are sad or troubling, we may tense our bodies and cross our arms over our hearts and curl up around our bellies to protect them, and then it is good to feel like we can move our bodies to counter-stretch and release that tension.

Sometimes the women don't know why they are drawn to the workshop and I need to be prepared for something from their history to surface during the day. We like to compartmentalize and think that abuse survivors are someone else, but most of us are carrying something. Even if it is not from our own lifetime or in our own conscious memory, we are affected by things that happened even generations ago that nobody talked about. When women come to their time to give birth, they are not only bringing their own experiences, but those of the long line of women who have gone before them, and all of the stories that they've heard about birth, and everything that they've internalized from the current birth culture. Maybe when they were born or their mother was born there was trauma that went unhealed. With the use of "twilight sleep" for all those decades, I worry that there were generations of women feeling the trauma trapped in their cells but they were robbed of the memories that would have at least made sense of the feelings. The doulas have to hold space for all of that, for the birthing woman and the baby. Birth-work is an honor and a privilege. I like to give the women who are doing this powerful work a day to explore all of that and to really feel into it because it is not something that you can learn from a textbook. If we can help survivors to feel empowered by birth, and not re-traumatized, and if the babies feel safe and loved from the beginning, then we can make huge shifts for the next generations.

For some, surviving means that they've put on their armor and put up walls to protect themselves. Fighting to survive puts you on the offensive which feels better than being on the defensive and feeling like being a victim. So feeling strong is better, but it is still not healed, and it is still a tool that you use to feel safe enough when your whole being is telling you that it is not really safe here. We tell ourselves stories to make the world make sense. If someone has their emotional wall up and I knock and ask to enter, trying to connect with them on a deeper level, they panic and go on lockdown. Some get stronger and make themselves look scary like the little kitten puffing up to look like a lion. I know that I am coming in peace, but they attack me to maintain distance because they have learned that it is dangerous to let anyone that close. Some turn and run away. Some people just give up and let everyone in to walk all over them and they don't even fight anymore. But that is surviving too. So I get people in my workshops that argue with me, reject me, and attack me and I have to hold space for that while keeping the other attendees comfortably above it all. Some people take a lot of breaks, tune out and ignore me. Some try to shock me as a way to test and see if I will reject them. I have to honor the ways in which each person has learned to feel safe. I know that I use different survivor tools at different times. But it is still hard to not go on the defensive when someone is on the offensive, and it is hard to not take it personally when I wrote the book and created the program.

So I have my own support network ready to pick me back up when I'm worn out. It takes a lot to hold space for all of that emotion while also being vulnerable and letting them see the real me, while being strong enough to not take it personally when they don't like what I'm trying to teach them. It would certainly be easier to give up and not even try to fight against these cultural patterns of abuse and violence at all, but I am so passionate about this work. I have gotten better about creating my own routine for keeping myself healthy and refilling my own pitcher so that I can continue to do this work. Part of it comes from recognizing when there is something that I still need to heal and not backing down from doing the work. I know when I need to just push through instead of turning around, giving up, or finding some way around it. I feel like I'm in that old song and I'm going on a bear hunt. I'll keep telling myself that I'm not afraid. I can't go over it, can't go under it, can't go around it, I guess I've got to go through it. (37) All of that can just feel like more work though, and some days it feels like I am still just getting started. Then I start singing that other folk song where the bear goes over the mountain and all that he can see is the other side of the mountain. Sometimes when we dive into the truth of why we really are hurting, we just find another story. Despite connecting all the dots, and recognizing the patterns, I still didn't know how to completely surrender. I felt like I had to always be on guard, using all of my tools to cope. It was like I was putting on energetic armor to feel protected, instead of actually being strong.

Like that airplane taking off, if we can just push through to the next level, we break through the clouds and there are good things waiting for us on the other side. I knew that if I could just let go, if I could really forgive, if I could learn to love myself, then I could let go and take that leap. I had learned that pain was not a punishment. I knew that my physical symptoms were just clues to follow so that I knew what emotional memory really needed attention. I was learning how to translate the messages that my body was sending me, instead of feeling like it hated me when I was in pain and had no idea why. If I could find my way and surrender into being my full self, then I would be able to do so much good in the world. The problem was that I wanted to help everyone and fix everything and I had no idea where to even start because it all seemed so big. I wanted to be able to let my guard down, but sometimes, I would just feel everything and it would be too much.

One night, I woke up from a dream that was so vivid and so detailed. I didn't know if it was symbolic or if I was supposed to write something about it because I am not usually given that many clear details in my dreams. I thought that maybe I was supposed to do some investigation or do more to prevent human trafficking because there were these women in a basement and I was trying to help them escape. I sat with them and we planned. I thought maybe it was a message to check on my friend, because the woman that I was sitting next to in the dream looked like one of my young friends from Godspell. But when I saw the news in the morning there was coverage of these women who had just escaped from the basement where they had been held for years after being abducted. One of them had the same curly hair as my friend. In that same moment while I was with them in my dreams, they had found the courage to finally break free. I wondered how many other women from around the globe had journeyed with them in their dreams that night.

I called the healer that I had met on retreat and she explained that my energy was so open and available to anyone who called for help. By wanting to save the world, I had basically hung a neon sign saying: "Free Help Available Here." When people called out for help, I would send them energy without even knowing that I was doing it. Having that dream be so vivid added to what I had felt when my brother's soul called out to mine. I wondered how many other times it had happened but I had not seen a clear explanation on the news. Maybe like this time, I was just so exhausted that I couldn't get out of bed. Maybe this explained those times when I had found myself crying and I didn't know the reason, I just knew that it felt huge. Maybe this explained some of my depression. My son would get like this too and he'd come home from school some days and just pass out on the couch, but he wasn't feverish or sick, just completely exhausted. The day that these women needed help I had a huge family party. I needed to host and cook and get the kids dressed and drive to the church, so it wasn't easy to function when I was so zapped. Some days, even with all the right tools, it is just too much to handle alone.

I asked this healer if she could teach me how to help others without draining my own energy. I wanted to be able to say "yes" when people needed help, like in this case when these women really needed a sisterhood, but I still needed to be able to function in my own life. I signed up for her class so that I could learn how to create boundaries and find balance. Unlike the business workshop that I had taken that was taught by a young man, this was taught by a mother who had learned how to balance her healing work with raising her children. She taught it as a year-long class because it would take us through each season and all of the anniversaries that can be a challenge as they bring up old wounds. We would be able to hold each other accountable and support each other as we grew.

As we learned to tune in to our own inner knowing, we also had to learn to tune out all of the background noise. I had always been good at school, but this class was completely different than anything I had ever studied. A big thing for me was learning to accept that there was no right answer. Each classmate had their own gifts and talents and their own way of seeing the world. There are so many ways that we can receive messages from the world, and from God, or the universe. Some of us see patterns, others see colors. Some hear words, some have dreams. Some have a thought pop into their head that they know is not their inner voice. Some see synchronicities in their world and learn to pay attention. Some people hear angels, and other people think they are crazy or just say that because they wish that they heard angels, too. In many ways, we were learning to tune back in the talents that we had as little girls that we were told to put away and pretend weren't there. Maybe we talked to our parents about our elaborate dreams in the morning, or had conversations with invisible friends, or saw angels, and we were told that it was just our imaginations. Maybe we saw the monsters and nobody believed us. Whatever the gifts, children are often told to ignore them and to act "normal." It is dangerous to stand out and to be different from your tribe. So we lose faith in our intuition, we stop trusting our gut reactions, and we stop trusting God. In this class, we spent a lot of time re-learning. It was always exciting to rediscover something that you used to know. It was like reconnecting with an old friend. We learned to accept our uniqueness as we healed old wounds from those traumatic moments when we were not heard or not believed and our trust was broken. As our physical symptoms quieted down, as each story was heard and validated and our bodies could again find balance, our talents blossomed.

As I walked back from the bus stop with the baby one day after the "big kids" went off to school, I noticed the blossoms on the burning bush. Those bushes are known for the fact that their leaves turn fiery red in the fall, and aren't called flowering bushes by landscapers like the ones with the white bridal veil or the big pink flowers. I always remember how old the hedge is because I planted the bushes when I was eight months pregnant with my middle child and I was excited to be out gardening and not stuck on bed rest like I had been with the twin pregnancy. But on this day years later, I saw its flowers for the first time. They easily escape notice because they are tiny and green and they blend in with the baby leaves in the spring. I realized in that moment, that whether we notice them or not, they still blossom.

Sometimes we need to stop comparing ourselves to others or to some ideal and stop clinging to some fantasy of being "normal." We need to let go of the life that we thought we were going to have and give ourselves enough space to grow so that we can create the life that we are meant to lead. Sometimes the plant that has unassuming flowers in the spring will burst forth in brilliant colors in the fall.

Things to think about:

- What are your hidden talents? When you were a little kid, what did you want to be when you grew up? What did you enjoy? What could you do that your family or the kids at school thought was weird?

- What things in your life are feeling like they are a little bit too comfortable? Maybe they are worn out and it is time for something new, but you are not ready to let go yet. What needs to be put to rest so that you can live fully?

- Make a list of your biggest triggers: the ones that make you want to run away, start fighting or just freeze. Include the Physical triggers like barking dogs, spiders, snakes, swimming, or heights, and the emotional ones like speaking in public, being interrupted or shushed, not being heard, feeling like someone is talking behind your back.

- Pick one trigger and practice using EFT (tapping) at home. Look up some videos for your specific triggers. Practice tapping with your kids when they need to learn to calm themselves down. Try tapping after they lose the game, before the big test, or when they fight with their friend over a toy.

- What stories did you tell yourself so that your life would make sense? Which stories are you ready to put back on the shelf? Which stories do you need to burn? If you could write a new story for your life, what would it be?

- How do you see your future self? What steps do you need to take to move closer to her? How can you start to create a life that resembles your vision?

Chapter 7: Connecting with Spirit

When a baby is born, they have what are called "soft spots" on the tops of their heads, right where the seventh energy center lies. I've often thought that it is not just because their heads need to be able to squish a bit to fit through the birth canal and push out into the world. I think there is also a connection to how the veil is so thin between the spiritual and the physical world at birth, and the baby is still living a little bit in both for a while, and those soft spots give them more direct access to their connection to the divine. I've heard some people call the seventh chakra the "umbilical cord to the divine." As we outgrow infancy and those soft spots close, we need to learn how to keep that connection vibrant. In meditation we can picture our energy going up to the light and being one with the Divine. Some of us have to do a lot of work to regain this ability as adults, so I am trying to help my children to maintain their connection so they do not have to do that work of rebuilding and repairing that relationship when they are older.

Those soft spots are open longer than you would think. They may not completely close until the baby is over a year and maybe even closer to two years old. This is partly why you need to be so careful to hold their heads when they are babies and to not shake them. Of course, you need to make sure that all of the baby's physical needs are met, but you also need to remember to help them stay emotionally, mentally and spiritually healthy and balanced, so they can continue to have faith and joy and peace. When there is a healthy flow of energy from your root all the way up to this crown chakra at the top of the head, there is a feeling of happiness and bliss. This can also be characterized as a feeling of love, but it is more of a universal love for all things, a love of beauty, and a love of life, not just love the way we think of it in human relationships.

When someone spends too much time in the 7th energy center and they are not in balance with all of the other parts of themselves, they can be described as a little too spacey. It is not good to be called a space cadet or to zone out when you are supposed to be doing something or listening to someone. But, it can feel lovely to be totally blissed out, "on cloud 9," in "7ᵗʰ heaven," or "in orbit." If this is blocked because you can't trust, you are mad at God, or the energy can't flow to this energy center because it is stuck in the lower chakras, you can seem aimless, distracted, or depressed. You might suffer from headaches or addictions and even paralysis and muscular symptoms. (30) I try to stay both connected to the divine and grounded in my everyday life at the same time, to be balanced in mind/body/spirit and to model how to do that for my kids. It's not always easy, but those moments when you need to remember your tools are actually the best times to teach your children, since I am sure that there will be times in their life when something difficult happens and they'll need to call on these techniques. I find that bedtime and long car trips are the times when I end up talking to my children about these deeper spiritual issues.

I was excited when I had worked my way through

healing the other chakras and could work on the seventh, which meant that I could focus on the color violet and on connecting to spirit. I love purple and I wear it every day (and as I heal I am learning to love all of the others colors, too) and I also love amethyst crystals and the smell of lavender which are also used to tune in to this energy. This (spiritual world) was my comfort zone (much more so than being in my body) and I thought that I had fewer wounds in this area. I was always happy with my connection to Spirit, the only problem was that I thought of Spirit as being up there and I was down here. I realized that I loved God so much, but I admired from afar, and I couldn't let God in. Why would God want to be with me when I was such a mess? I needed inspiration, to be inspired, to be in spirit. I needed to learn to follow that inspiration and let the Spirit guide me to where I needed to be and give me the courage to truly live my soul's purpose. I had always gathered my courage while hiding behind my wall, which is a great tool for survivors of abuse and trauma to use to navigate the world. I was ready to learn to be held by a loving, caring God, and to let God be strong for me. I didn't need to find the courage; I needed to let myself trust that with God on my side I didn't need courage. To be held takes a lot of surrender though, a lot of letting go, and like the girl on the snow tube, sometimes although we know that it is time to let go, we hold on even tighter to the things that we have always known.

I was nervous about starting the energy healing class because it seemed so far outside of my world and I didn't know if it would clash with my religious beliefs and my family traditions. In the very first class, we started with a meditation and I had no idea what I was supposed to do and no way of knowing if I was doing it right. I used to be good at school, but in this class I felt so far behind the others. Feeling stupid is a huge trigger for me, but I worked through it. I knew the teacher and I knew that she did good work, so I decided to trust her. In that moment, she used an expression that was straight out of one of my favorite folk songs from church that I had been singing my entire life. I asked her if she knew the song, and she said she'd never heard it. I asked her if she knew the bible verse, and she did not. She said that they weren't her words; she had just given me the message. It was from Spirit. It was just for me. It was to bring me comfort.

Before I met this teacher, I had been studying Carolyn Myss' Energy Anatomy books and had recently found another book of hers that was framed around the writings of St. Theresa of Avila. (20, 38) After reading

Myss' *Entering the Castle*, I went and found a translation of St. Theresa of Avila's book *The Interior Castle* that she wrote in her convent in 1577 based on a vision that she had of a crystal castle made up of seven mansions. (39) It brought me great comfort to know that this Catholic mystic could hear God the way that I did. St. Theresa used the imagery of going through these 7 spiritual levels of going deeper into your soul (interior of the castle) until you are at one with God and that is where you will reach what she calls the "peace of soul" and find healing. (39) St. Theresa was said to go into a trancelike state when she experienced what she called "the flight of the spirit," which she said was like a "flashing comet." (39) She described it as a feeling of ecstasy, and that just seemed kind of inappropriate for a woman, especially a nun, to describe feeling such joy and pleasure. In my world, women were not allowed to feel pleasure. We were supposed to suffer and to sacrifice. But in Theresa's case she was just so in love with Jesus that the priests decided that it was okay (kind of) but then they made her describe how she did it and write out instructions for them follow. In *Entering the Castle*, Myss gives us modern ideas on how to apply St. Theresa's spiritual practice of going within and connecting with your own soul on a deeper level. (38)

I love the way that St. Theresa wrote and the down to earth way in which she connects with her readers. It was refreshing to find that someone who was so good at being "spaced out" could also be so grounded. Sometimes I would feel sorry for her, because she uses so many words to describe something that is much easier for us today. When describing the "flight of the spirit" and the sound that it makes, she struggles to find the right description. When I felt it for the first time in my meditation practice, it sounded just like a helicopter inside my brain. Now we can use Velcro as a way to describe how negativity can stick to you. When you have victim energy, maybe it is like the softer side of Velcro, but it attracts that rougher side and the two are made to stick together. The way St. Theresa describes how the lost souls look is a very clear visual for me because of that cartoon with the mermaid which I've seen so many times. Although I feel like some things have gotten easier for us to describe so that people instantly know what we mean, it is interesting to see how much has not changed, and how a lot of the symbols that we use have stayed the same for hundreds and even thousands of years. (39) Theresa uses butterflies, and spirals, and water, and a gold locket that only you can open to reveal the jewel inside to describe some of the ways in which her spirituality and her relationship with God works.

Theresa says that many people stumble into the castle through prayer, at the 4th level, with a heart connection. They love feeling close to God but don't know how to stay there in that heart space. I love how this is a Catholic from the 1500s and when she tunes in to the different levels they align with the ancient teachings about chakras or energy centers. The 4th chakra is the heart chakra. When she talks about the "flight of the spirit," she says that it is not really like hearing with your ears, but it is like your spirit rushes out the top of your head, and that is how I have heard healers describe it when telling you to bring your energy up and out through your crown, or your 7th chakra. It was perfect to find these descriptions that showed me that people from every background, various cultural traditions, and different religions have all learned to use the energy centers of their bodies or the seven levels of spiritual healing as a way to connect their spirit and their soul with the Divine.

So after we stumble in to the castle and feel that our soul can be close to God (Theresa calls it the "sweetness"), then we actually want to go and do the work to remove the obstacles and the things of the world that are keeping us distracted and busy and stuck in the first three levels. Everything that she talks about when describing the work that you have to do to clean up all of those worldly attachments reminds me of the work that I had been doing on clearing the blocks in my energy centers. It makes me feel better that she mentions how she had it easy living in a convent and having enough time to really meditate deeply because she had people to take care of her so that she had so much time to rest and pray. She gives so much credit to the people who are living out in the world and trying to run businesses and households and raise children and who still try to be in a close relationship with God. She knew that those people in her community were busy earning the money and buying and preparing the food to take care of their families, and it was no small thing when they also found time to care for their souls.

The Holy Spirit is often described as a helper. After Mary Magdalene found the resurrected Jesus at the tomb, He went on to appear to the other apostles. After He ascended to heaven, Jesus sent the Holy Spirit to guide them and comfort them. There are seven gifts of the Holy Spirit including things like courage and faith. In his letters to the early Christians, St. Paul described how we each receive what we need and we each have different gifts. Some people have the gift of healing and can lay hands on the sick, some know the right words to say in the moment, some have spiritual discernment, and others can perform miracles. (40)

I am learning to be able to tell the difference between when my guidance (call it having a good idea) comes from my own intuition or inner knowing or gut reactions (which can be thought of as your epigenetics or your ancestors giving you advice) verses when it comes from inspiration, which is help from the Spirit. Sometimes I get very clear instructions and I know that they are from God, because they are for my good and they move me towards my higher purpose, but they are things that I would never dream up myself. It also helps to be familiar with those songs and verses so that I know when it sounds like something that God would say, or when I am being deceived. Sometimes someone would come to mind that I needed to pray for, and I didn't want to alarm them just in case it was nothing but I'd try to contact them to check in and see how they were doing. I used to worry when they didn't respond to my messages right away, but then they'd usually get back to me in a few days and apologize for the delay, as they had been sick in bed or at the hospital, or they'd been sitting with a dying friend. I've learned to listen to these instructions and just send the prayers right away and not worry about the details, trusting that more information would come if it was needed. Sometimes the instructions are about something that I need to be doing. Usually these are actions that are farther outside my comfort zone and I don't really want to do them, and in those moments I can become like a child again, whining that I don't feel like doing that chore and I'd rather just play.

Some people like to think of Jesus as a friend who is always with you, always by your side, carrying you in times of trouble. It is like when you have a tragedy that shakes you to your core and you don't know how you will even be able to put one foot in front of the other, and then you find that somehow you made it here anyway. He is with you in the times when you need to find the courage to step into the unknown and don't know how you can do it alone. Sometimes he walks with you and encourages you and you just don't feel so alone. Sometimes he carries you and only leaves one set of footprints. (13) I've also met people who are not even Christians, but they deeply believe in the Christ light, which is the energy that connects the Divine in the universe to the Divinity in you and is the light that is always within you, filling you and strengthening you for the journey.

Some people don't like to come to God through the story of a man. Many people have been hurt at the hands of men and don't want to think of the Divine as anything resembling humans. Some are so hurt by what patriarchy has done to the church over the centuries that they need to be distanced from the institutions and the shackles of a single religion. Many are still traumatized from the burning times (that are not that far back in our history) or the crusades and they just can't understand (rightly so) how people can torture and murder in the name of God. They want no part of that God. Since I was a little girl, it's been like I can feel Jesus crying when hurtful things are done in the name of God or in His church. When faced with abuse and trauma and oppression, distance is an excellent tool, so you can't blame or shame anyone who has chosen to move away from the church and is seeking their spirituality in their own way.

It can make sense to just bypass religion and tradition and get straight to that oneness with God. For some, even that word holds too many painful memories, so they don't even use the word God; they say Spirit or Source, the Creator or the Universe. Some just tune in to the Light and to Love. But God *is* Love. Many people who are tuning in to that Love are more aligned with God than someone who is talking about God from a place of blaming, and shaming, or while hating their neighbor. We need to stop fighting about the labels and start working together to bring more love into the world and start taking care of each other. We need to stop arguing over nouns. We should stop waging wars over titles and labels and invisible lines in the sand. We need to look beyond appearances and see the true nature of people. We need to react to their intentions even when we are not familiar with their customs or their traditions. If we can do the work to heal by starting to see the ways in which we are using our own survivor tools to keep ourselves safe (by being strong, looking tough, creating distance, and striking first) then we can start to see those tools when others use them and see past that to their underlying fears, and then we can send them some love and understanding.

When I started doing more of this deep meditation and connecting to God more personally, I was given the gift of being able to more clearly see past people's actions and words. I could see to the heart of their intentions. I thought of my cat, who as a tiny kitten was so traumatized by the veterinarian who stupidly put him in a cage next to a dog while he was already hallucinating from the medications that he was given for his surgery. The vet actually tried to reassure me by saying that they put a towel over his cage and that my cat couldn't see the dog. I am not an animal expert, but even I know that my cat could hear and smell the dog, never mind sense his presence. When I called to ask how my cat was doing, they couldn't even give me an update because he was attacking the staff whenever they went near the cage. When I got there he had his fur puffed up to look like a ferocious lion and was hissing his warning, but as soon as I opened the cage he jumped into my arms and meowed, and in his kitty language asked me to just take him home. So now, when someone is attacking me (usually verbally) or acting tough or putting their guard up, I can see past those behaviors that are masking their fear to the scared little kitten underneath that is their true self.

There is actually a lot of research about how hugs can heal. Loving touch can reduce your stress hormones, improve your immunity and help your wounds to heal faster. (5) Just like when my kitty jumped into my arms to go home where he felt safe and loved, love can calm the savage beast and turn them back into cute kittens. Baby rats in the lab that had undergone medical trauma could have their stress pathways rewired by being placed in the cages with nurturing mothers. But even though the attention and comforting touch improved their health, they found that the effects of the trauma were inheritable in the rat's epigenetics for a few generations. (6)

When a toddler starts taking a swing at you with their little fists, it is not always easy to remain calm. It reminds me of that mom who told me to not have a reaction when the nursing baby bites your nipple because it would scare them, but I never quite managed to not yelp and cringe. It is easier to work with these behaviors at the infant and toddler stage when it is much easier to remember that they are your precious baby than if you wait until they are taller than you. If your child prefers flight to fight, then it is also easier to work on it before they can run faster than you. The early years are the best time to connect deeply with your children, teach them about unconditional love, and show them how to ground themselves. Practicing staying present and helping them to learn how to calm themselves down in the moment can be a great way for you to practice it yourself.

When they hit at two years old, you can easily let your mind jump to the future and think that they'll still be doing this at twenty years old and then envision all of the repercussions of that and blow it way out of proportion. When they run away and hide behind the curtains, you picture them running off and being abducted and living on the streets. You need to stay present and be with them in this moment that is making them fight you or flee from you, and realize that they are learning to handle emotions that feel too big. The problem is often that many of us did not get to learn how to ground ourselves and be present when we were small, so we are just trying to figure it out now after years of forming habits based on jumping straight into our stress response. We also don't have a lot of great models for a healthier response in our mainstream society. They market to our fears and show us a continuous stream of news reports that keep us traumatized by worrying and waiting for the worst to happen. I knew that I didn't have the right tools and after noticing my regular tendency to jump right into blame and shame, I switched gears and started looking for new mentors. I found things that I could try right now, and implement into my regular routine. I learned alongside my kids, and we grew together.

I used to say that my kids were so manipulative and the moms at the play group would be so shocked and say that I couldn't say such things about my babies. But I wasn't saying it with any disrespect. I was really quite impressed with how well they could manipulate any situation to meet their own needs. Usually they want something like more food, more attention, or more freedom. Just before she died, my cousin's biological field research was showing how even baby birds lie to their mothers. When they were already fed they would cry loudly saying "I'm starving" and push to the front to get more food and attention than their siblings. We are all designed with this imperative drive to survive. We don't need to deny it or be ashamed of it, it is just our biology. But I am getting tired of always being in survival mode. I am tired of carrying so much worry about being fed, when logically I know that I am blessed to have a full refrigerator and pantry, and I don't need to be so fearful all of the time. God says to look to the lilies of the field that don't work or try hard or worry, they just turn their faces to the sun and God provides all that they need. (41) We are supposed to rest in that assurance and trust that everything that we need will be provided if we just learn to receive. It is exhausting to always have your guard up. I am ready to be nurtured and cherished. I just don't know how to relax into that. So a community like my Red Tent women's circle gives me a place where I feel safe to practice receiving. It still takes courage to push outside of that comfort zone and start to break those old habits.

But if we each take a tiny step forward, together we can start to make a shift.

I draw inspiration from many sources as I continue to create my vision of a peaceful and healthy world where everyone knows that they are well cared for and loved. The whole world seems kind of big though, so I create this feeling as much as I can in my own home for now. I guess it makes sense to start with a spark and then let it spread from there. (That's actually the message we received on a chocolate wrapper at our very first gathering of the Red Tent and we keep it in our collection of sacred items.) I want my kids to know what peace and security feels like. I want them to notice when they need to go into survival mode, I don't want it to be their default setting. Then, after the stressful event is over (after having listened to their intuition and trusted their gut and fought back or ran to safety or played dead) their biochemical stress response can relax back to baseline. When they experience something traumatic, I don't want them to pretend that it is fine. I want them to notice it. I want them to shake it off and tap out those yucky feelings. I want them to know how to create ceremony and acknowledge it and let it go, so that it doesn't need to take root in their bodies and start to blossom into disease down the road. I don't want them to just survive, I want them to thrive. Wanting it so badly for my kids, made me realize how much I needed it too.

As I cleared all of my old emotional wounds and checked things off of my healing to-do list, working through each energy center, my physical symptoms went away. I no longer needed medication for asthma and allergy. I didn't take painkillers for joint pain anymore. I stopped saying that I had a bad back and I didn't need to have the heated massage cushion that plugged into the outlet in my car just so I could sit long enough to drive to an appointment. I enjoyed eating real food. I danced. I sang. I hiked mountains. I played with my kids. All of those symptoms made sense given my history, all of the things that happened in my childhood, and the stories that I was carrying for my family that had gone unhealed for generations. It had become a pattern of victims and abusers in which everyone suffers. By acknowledging the emotional pain and bringing the secrets into the light, I was able to release the hold that they had on me, and as they lost their power, my body didn't need to carry them anymore. More importantly, I felt like my kids wouldn't have to continue to do this much work for another generation. I could see the healing spreading seven generations forward, and seven generations back. (42)

When I read St. Theresa's book *The Interior Castle*, she talked about going through similar steps of releasing the hold that the physical world has on your soul. The way she shows us how to move through the seven mansions, and how to reach the inner mansions and become one with the light, is similar to rebalancing your seven chakras and working through the seven stages of spiritual healing that Myss describes. As you move through self-knowledge and awakening, you become aware of the things of this world that are keeping you busy, clouding your vision and hiding your inner light. In Theresa's castle imagery she calls the bad thoughts and negativity *"lizards"* that are crawling all over the exterior of the castle and inhabiting the first mansions, and keeping you distracted and busy battling your demons. Getting rid of these lizards lets you see the castle underneath all that commotion. (39)

If you realize that these *"lizards"* have no real power and they are just distractions, you can start to loosen the hold that the cares of this world have over you. We worry about what our friends think, we worry about how we look to everyone else, and we strive and struggle for success and esteem. But worldly things will never satisfy. They do not last. Everything that we need is within. So we can also choose to just stop battling those demons, stop shooing those lizards away, and just walk past them and go within. We still need to eat, we still need to sleep, we still need to put the laundry in the washing machine and then the dryer, but we can start to do those things with a grateful heart, knowing that they are necessary for this physical reality, but they are not the most important thing and should not consume all of our time and energy. We do not need to worry and occupy our minds with what everyone thinks about us, we can stop looking for greener pastures and we can just be satisfied. We can just be in this present moment and stop believing that all the good moments are off in the bright future or nostalgically resting in the past. We can make every task that we do and every bite of food that we consume into a prayer of thanksgiving. It is so simple, but it is not easy.

As I read Theresa's description of the lizards I felt the book dropping out of my hands as I suddenly had this vision come over me. I saw my mother on her spiritual quest. Although she did not grow up Catholic, she had been seeking her true path and had converted during college (at great cost to her relationship with her own mother) and then she had gone into a convent

where the nuns then told her that God had other
plans for her. She went on to get married and have 5
children, including me, but I think she still sought the
solace of retreating into a sanctuary. In my vision, she
came out of cloister into the world of raising children
and battling the demons of family patterns and she got
pulled down by all of those lizards and was sinking
into the blackness of all of those spiritual attacks. I
watched as all that thick, black, yucky stuff from our
family history and her early medical trauma was
pulling her under. What I really needed to see and to
acknowledge was how in that moment, despite all of
her fears, she found that particular kind of courage that
only comes from motherhood and she used what was
left of her strength to push me up and out of that mire
onto the next level of the mansion. She fell back into
the darkness of depression and for so many years I was
looking backwards and trying to save her but that kept
all of my energy focused on fighting those demons.
Whenever I tried to turn and look forward towards the
light to heal for my family, I felt like I was abandoning
her. I felt like I wasn't strong enough to go on alone. I
was stuck there for a long time. This vision showed me
that by standing up and walking into the light, I was
actually honoring her sacrifice. I knew in that moment
that I would be able to help my family more by moving

into that place of grace, where I would be able to feel
God's love and learn to trust.

I needed to take that pebble from my shoe, leave
it there as a marker for my mother, and then move
forward on my new road. I looked for those moments of
inspiration to lead me. When God put an opportunity
on my path, I knew that it was time for me to gather
my courage to say "yes" and take that first step. I had
to hold on to my vision and just fake it until I made
it there. Some leaders teach that you should follow
your desires. But some of us can't even imagine being
allowed to desire beautiful things. We make do with
what we need. We use serviceable dishes and we wear
decent clothes that don't attract too much attention.
We eat the apples from the seconds' bin that are a little
bit funny-looking, but still taste just as good. We don't
bother wanting something more because then the lack
of it would hurt too much. It's kind of ugly and it could
be a source of more shame, but take a moment to think
of a time recently when you were feeling jealous and
resentful. What is it that the other person had that
you secretly wanted? Who was it that you wished you
could be? Use those moments to let the little light-bulb
switch on and start adding those images to your mental
vision board (or create an actual vision board if you are

crafty). Pay attention to those people that you kind of hate a little bit because they have something that you secretly wish that you had. You don't really hate them, it's just that you would love to be like them, but can't even picture that, so you push it away.

Stay in that moment a little longer than is comfortable and pinpoint which aspect of their life is appealing to you. Maybe you don't really care what they are wearing or what they are eating, but you would just love the chance to sit for a moment in a chair in an outdoor café and turn your face to the sun and watch the world go by without anyone pulling on your shirt or asking you questions or making you feel like you will never be able to give enough. If you think about it, that woman that you are looking at probably has her own set of real problems and if you got to know her you would realize that you don't really want her life after all. I often see those young women who look like they are so unencumbered, and for just a second I kind of long for those days again before I remember that when I was their age I was looking longingly at the pregnant bellies and the mothers with babies in their arms and wanting so badly to be a mother myself. So now my children are here with me and I don't have to wonder about if and when they will come to be a part of my story. That brings a certain peace to my heart, but sometimes I am still longing for just a second of quiet so that I can remember who I am above and beyond this role of mother. If this sounds like something that you need sometimes too, then maybe you can sneak away and recreate that café moment for yourself before you go back home with gratitude for all of the people that need so much of you.

As we have learned from social media and holiday parties, it is dangerous to compare our insides (the depth of our true feelings) to someone else's outsides (the tiny bit of themselves that they let show on the surface). Maybe what you desire comes at a price that you are not willing to pay. When someone asks how you lost weight they somehow never want to hear that you ate organic veggies and exercised. I would love to have a gorgeous manicure and look more polished in general, but then I would start pulling weeds in my garden and ruin it anyway, so I know it wouldn't really work for me. One time I commented on someone's beautiful nails, but then when I heard her whole story of how much time she spent keeping them like that and the number of things that she had to avoid doing to maintain them, I knew that just wasn't going to be at the top of my list and I wasn't so jealous anymore. If we start to ask real questions and create real connections, we can make real choices about how to take steps forward towards our own personal vision of living a life that brings us real joy.

I had one of those *Magdalena Moments* calling to me when I saw beautiful pictures of women in natural settings. I secretly longed to be able to see myself as beautiful even though my nickname growing up was "Ugly" and the boys that would hang out with me in private wouldn't be seen with me in public, and even the moms at the party didn't think to include me in the group picture with all the ladies. I wanted to have photos of my outsides that somehow showed my inner beauty. I had been doing so much work on my fear of being seen and this could be the reward. But it was hard to let go. I asked my friend who is a doula and a birth photographer to go with me to the park to take the pictures because I knew that she'd be able to hold space for me as I did this healing and this coming out of my cocoon.

I found a dress that reminded me of the princess prom dress that I never had. I bought the dress just for me, to feel like an empowered goddess, not for any official occasion or to impress a date. It's funny how our fantasies play out quite differently in the real world than in our visions. It's kind of like comparing the realities of dating and relationships verses watching a romantic comedy. I met my friend at the park by the river at sunset (when the lighting is at the best angle) and we headed out to take some photos. We did a few shots in regular clothes to use on my website and then I changed into the dress. I had spent a lot of time doing my hair so that it would look perfect, but then the wind was blowing it in my face and it became a tangled mess. The mosquitoes and flies were eating me alive and as I skipped through the meadow in my bare feet I suddenly felt something and looked down to see that I had stepped on a dead bird; so much for feeling glamorous. But then I went into the river and walked along the stepping stones and thought of all those steps that I had taken to get here. As I walked and walked, I kept feeling like something was missing and then I realized that it was my shame.

I couldn't wait for her to send me the pictures, and then she sent one in an email to tide me over. She said that it came out beautifully. When I opened the file I cried. I was so disappointed. I didn't look like a goddess. I looked like my grandmother. But she was old. I hadn't realized how many wrinkles I had already. She sent another that made me realize that although I had felt so proud about losing the pregnancy weight, I was really not that thin anymore. Basically, I had to accept that I could buy the prom dress, but I couldn't go back to being a teenager. It was kind of unfair; I should've learned to have some self-esteem when I was younger. It would have been easier then. Looking at the real me was painful. I felt bad for all the people who had to look at me. I knew that this habit of negative self-talk was ingrained from years of internalizing the voices of my abusers, but I still hadn't learned how to shut it off. My friend from my energy healing class was always asking me if I would ever talk to another woman the way that I talked to myself. I would never judge anyone else as harshly. I tried to take a step back from my fears about how the world sees me, and my fears about never being enough. I tried to talk to myself like a friend. Over time, the pictures started to grow on me.

Amongst all of the pictures of *me*, she sent one photograph that was totally *Magdalena*. I talked about it in my Red Tent women's circle. I shared that I'd had this vision of Magdalena and I had been trying to find the bridge that would get me from where I am to where she is. I still couldn't quite believe that it was me in that picture, too. I kept seeing her as my future self, but here she was, now. As I passed around my phone so everyone could see the photo, one woman pointed out that those stones on the side of the river were actually an old abandoned bridge. I hadn't even thought about that. Another woman mentioned that it looked like the crumbling tower in Tarot. I'm not very familiar, but I guess sometimes you see this symbol when you need your old world to crash down so you can build a new life on more solid ground. And another woman shared with me that the Magdalene is not actually named after a city, it means "the watchtower." The watchtower means someone who is strong and courageous; she is the one who sees further. I guess I didn't need to find a bridge after all, since I had just gotten into the river and started stepping from stone to stone. I didn't need to wait to be rescued. I didn't need to build anything. I didn't need to take a leap. I didn't need to learn how to fly. I could just get in and start walking across. I could walk and walk.

The flying imagery is still valid though, because in that moment, surrounded by my sisterhood, I felt like I was finally able to spread my wings. St. Theresa talks about how, when we are frightened of everything and afraid to make progress, we kind of wish that someone else would make the journey for us. (39) When she said this I actually laughed out loud because it reminded me of when I was stuck in my nursing chair with two newborns and I could send my husband to the kitchen for food or send him to change a baby, but then when I was too tired to do anything at all I'd ask him if he could go pee for me too so I didn't have to get up. Sometimes on our healing journey we get tired and a little whiny and just wish that someone could do this for us so we don't have to anymore. But some things you just have to do yourself. St. Theresa did say that when we do this work it helps others to do the same, which also happens to sound a lot like that Marianne Williamson quote at the beginning of Godspell about how when we let our light shine it gives permission for others to do the same. (20) St. Theresa says that it is encouraging when we see that trials that seem impossible to us are possible for others and "their flight makes us try to soar, like nestlings taught by the elder birds." (39, p.39) I thought that my cousin would love that imagery with the baby birds. I thought of that butterfly sitting on the branch and preparing for flight. And that word "soar" makes me think less of the struggle to take off and fly and more of surrendering to the joy of floating on the wind.

After you develop and grow, you need to take all

those things that you've learned along the way and use them to build your cocoon, die to your old self, learn to go within and listen to your intuition. Then, after you have transformed, you can emerge as a beautiful butterfly and stretch your wings in the sunshine. And then one day when you know the time is right, ready or not you need to just look forward at the view and leap; there is no need to look back at your own wings. When you are busy doing work that is aligned with your soul purpose, when you are feeding your babies or helping your neighbors or teaching the children or going to work to support your family there is no time to worry or to be embarrassed and ashamed. There are so many things that will distract you and dissuade you from taking the path that your soul is meant to follow. When you see someone else succeeding or relaxing, you think it will be easier to walk down their path than to clear the way for a new road of your own. When you listen to those voices that tell you that you don't deserve love, or that you are not enough, then it keeps you from hearing the voice that is telling you that you are loved and that you don't need to be enough because you are never alone. If you can't see your own beauty, you hide from others the beauty that is shining from your soul.

As you work through acknowledging and accepting

yourself at each energy center (from your roots in your culture and your family, to your self-esteem and creativity, to your identity and individuality, to finding balance at the heart of it all, to fully expressing yourself and holding space for your vision and finding inspiration for the journey,) you need to integrate each of the new changes as you stand taller and let the energy flow through your full self. At the point of finding fullness in the 7th chakra, when you connect to spirit and find your own true inspiration, you can start to experience what some call ascension symptoms. This is because when you have done so much healing for your spirit and your soul, sometimes your biology takes a while to catch up. If there are places where the stories are still hurting, they can continue to process while you dream at night or come to mind more often during your day. You can journal and meditate and ask to receive the messages, and then create ceremony to let them be put to rest. If your body is still holding on to something physically, you might have some aches and pains or tingling that brings your awareness to those parts. Use those symptoms as a call for more attention and send them love. Pushing out of the cocoon comes with growing pains, and leaves you with some stretch marks. Sometimes you need to pause, let a little light come in the cracks, and let yourself get used to how bright it is before you fully come out into the light and turn your face to the sun. But as the saying goes: *when you finally turn your face to the sun, the shadows fall behind you.*

I am still adjusting to the light. I am still learning to surrender to the larger plan. As I started to say "no" to being made to play the victim, I began to notice my survivor tools more clearly. These are the skills that bring me so much pride because they are what got me this far. I am great at planning and being prepared for anything. I am good in a crisis and I can roll with it and just wing it when things don't go as planned. I am hardworking and I don't quit. I am a perfectionist. I study and I research and I strategize. But I am starting to see how much all of this preparation and being in control is really a reaction to not being able to trust that someone will take care of me. As I learn to envision a healthy and joyful future, I realize that I cannot always create that for myself. Sometimes when I am working so hard to manifest what I have thought up on my own, I need to remember that maybe the real journey is in the not knowing. Maybe after healing the old wounds and stepping fully into my true self, I need to then surrender to something that is even better than something that I can think up on my own. In all those workshops on creating your vision and on following your desires, it started to be obvious that I would need to listen to something other than my own inner voice. St. Theresa says that God will give us even more than we know how to desire. Maybe it is time for me to see if God's plan for my life is even better than my own.

Things to think about:

- Inspiration: How are you letting spirit guide you on your journey?

- Can you trust that the unknown path may be even better than the path you planned to take? What can you do today that will help you relax into not knowing? Try allowing yourself to surrender to small pleasures first. Look for the opportunities that are put on your path and say "yes" even if you don't know where it will lead. Look for signs that you are loved and cared for abundantly.

- Give yourself permission to *think* less and *love* more. Find things to be grateful for every day.

- Be empowered to transform into your true self, the person that you were always meant to be before you got distracted and discouraged.

- What do you need to create in your life so that you feel safe to come out of your cocoon? What are some small self-care routines that you can try at home so that you can start to crack open your cocoon and let a little light in? How can you let a little joy into your life? What safe places do you have where you can practice letting your light shine and giving permission for others to do the same?

- When you are ready to spread your wings, don't forget to enjoy the view.

Epilogue

Mary Magdalene was the one who stayed at the foot of the cross when all but one of the others went to hide. She was the one who saw further and was the witness to the resurrection. She encouraged the other disciples to move beyond their fears to spread the good news after they had received the fruits of the spirit. After helping to start the entire movement of Christianity in the world, she was slandered and became hated by some of the very people that she had tried so hard to save. (13) When I started on my own healing journey, I simply wanted to stop being in physical pain every day. I knew that keeping secrets was what made people sick, whether it was lying to yourself about how you really feel, or being ashamed of your truth. I searched for meaning and I investigated to find the root cause of my pain and I turned over the rocks to see what was hiding underneath. I didn't know how much it would get me hated.

In the play *Enemy of the People* by Henrik Ibsen, we see how sometimes the people just don't want to know what is really going on beneath the surface and they are not pleased when you bring the story out into the light. (43) That play was written over a century ago, and I had read it many times with my students and I understood this concept really well in theory. Still, I had no way to know how much it would hurt to really feel the extent to which our culture blames the victim. We are impressed when the mastermind gets away with the crime, and we only think of criminals as losers when they get caught. We like things to stay private, behind closed doors, where we don't have to decide what to do about them. We are told to mind our own business. We are taught not to tell, not to snitch, not to squeal, and not to be the tattle-tale. "Loose lips sink ships." (44) But despite all of this cultural training, I started to wonder why the abuser is not thought of as the bad guy. Why is the victim the enemy of the family? Why do we punish the one who stands up and says that this has gone too far?

It is no wonder that the fear of speaking in public is a universal fear, especially for women. Our bodies start to put up red flags and scream "danger" and throw us into fight or flight mode and we turn red in the face. We get kind of nauseous, our hearts race, and our palms sweat as we dare to stand out in the crowd. As women, we can relate to the Magdalene because since childhood we've been told not to take up too much space and to apologize for existing. God forbid we show that we are stronger or smarter or better than a man. We need to keep watch and see further and be strong, because we are the mothers and the healers and the teachers. But those are far from our only jobs. Women work in so many places and in so many ways out in the world in addition to the work that we do in our homes and families. Whether we are in an office or on a construction site, women are often the ones who strategize and find ways to make sure that everyone's needs are met. Women get things done. And when it is time and enough is enough, we stand up and we break the silence.

I had been working on picking up all the pieces of myself that I had abandoned along the way because in the moment I had not known how to love that part of myself. There was my three year old self who was not heard when she cried "monster" and the little girl who needed a mommy but her mother couldn't get out of bed. As a mother now I can go back to those stories with compassion and understanding. At the time I had no way of knowing how hard it can be to survive that postpartum period. Now it makes sense to me that I couldn't convince her to get up. I would see that little girl who always needed a secret hiding place in the woods in my dreams, and during meditation I went to find her in that place that I knew so well, and I brought her back here to live with me now in my sanctuary by the waterfall.

In some traditions they call this work soul retrieval, as you go and find the parts of yourself that you have left behind somewhere. I could journey to find those pieces of myself in meditation, when I had a healer holding space for me so that I felt safe and protected. I needed to know that they would make sure that I found my way back to the present and that they would help me to integrate the changes into my life. For me, it helps to understand the story so that I can love those parts of myself, and then reintegrate them into who I am now. But in all my healing work, there was one piece of myself that I could never pick up because it was too heavy. I could love all those pieces of myself as a little girl, but my teenage self was so broken and she felt like it was all her fault and I couldn't go and feel her pain again. I just locked her away and kept going through the motions of having a regular life. I'm so thankful that I found a friend in my healing class that could help give me the strength to finally reach down and pick her up off of that apartment floor where I had left her when I turned my back and walked away.

I wrote an essay (or a poem or a fairy tale, I think they call it "creative nonfiction" now if you refuse to pick a genre) about that energy work that finally helped me to become whole again. I wrote it for all of the victims of abuse and trauma. I wrote it for everyone who is affected in so many ways by living in this rape culture. I felt stronger having integrated my past self and my future vision into my current reality, but then I didn't know what to do with that. I prayed for guidance, but then it's funny how much I dragged my feet when I was led to stand up and speak my truth in public. I believe that we all need to stand up against injustice, but then I kind of want someone else to go first and I'll just join in. I drag my feet because I don't really want to be the leader, but then that song that I'd been singing in church since I was a little girl came to mind and I remembered that I don't need to lead. It is the one that talks about how you hear Him calling in the night and you basically say "I guess I'll go, if you lead me." I know I have to go for all the people that need someone to hold them. I will hold them in my heart. (45)

My friend shared with me that she was going to a "Take Back the Night®" event in her state and I realized that I had been meaning to go to one for over twenty years and hadn't gotten up the courage yet. (46) I thought I'd look to see if there was one happening in my area. I found one, but then I put it out of my mind because it was almost an hour away and it was on a school night. I sat bolt upright in the middle of the night, woken out of a deep sleep with the very clear instruction that I *would* go and that I would read the essay that I had written a few months ago, which until that moment was tucked away in my journal and was never intended to be shared. This idea was not something that I would think up on my own, which is how I know when the instructions are coming from another source and not just my mind running through my to-do list in the night. The brat that I can be sometimes actually argued with God in this moment and silently explained that there was no way that I could do that, we were just too busy. Every day I open my family calendar and there are multiple places to be and my husband and I have logistics planning sessions on the porch after bedtime each night to see who can drive where and how to get everybody to where they need to be. My kids complain when I'm on the phone or texting but I point out to them that I'm just coordinating with the other moms to get them to the activities in which they want to participate. But when I opened my calendar this time, that evening was completely free. So I penciled it in. (I know I use an electronic calendar now, but that's still the expression, and I typed a question mark.) This partial-submission or lukewarm commitment was apparently not good enough to satisfy the boss, because the next night I was clearly told that in the morning I would email the organizer and tell her that I was coming. Oh, that's a good one. Apparently God knows how much I hate to let people down after I've actually committed to be somewhere.

So I sent the email and I asked her if it would be okay if I read something. I had timed it and done a practice read-through while I waited in my minivan one afternoon in between appointments, and it was about ten minutes long. Although there was an hour on the schedule of events for participants to share their stories, I didn't want to take more than my fair share of the available time. When I sent the email I was hoping that she would tell me that it was too long or too much of a bother. She said that she would love to have me read it. So I wrote to my Red Tent sisters and I asked for someone to go with me for emotional support. Finally someone said that they would go with me. She said that she was waiting and hoping that someone else would go because she didn't want to be out in public at a big event, but then she didn't want to leave me hanging. I told her that I totally understand hoping that someone else will do it. I picked her up at her house and on the drive there, when I was freaking out and whining about having to go, she mentioned that I was the one who wanted to go, not her. I told her that I didn't really *want* to go, I was *told* to go. I'm embarrassed to admit this in fear of sounding like a reluctant child who finally does their chores but with a big, loud sigh and some serious eye-rolling. But I share this in the hopes that you'll understand that Magdalena Moments are not always about saying "yes" to the things that you want, they're about learning to trust that you are part of a larger purpose, even if you can't yet see where your puzzle piece fits.

So ready or not, we said "yes" and we went. I had only shared my story in small rooms and in small

circles of women. This event was taking place in an
open air amphitheater with seats reaching up the hill
and stretching out into a huge park with the skyline
of the city in the background. There were mounted
policemen, city officials, politicians and professors and
more importantly, I noticed that a lot of them were
men. The organizer told me when I got there that one
other woman wanted to share something and then I
would speak. I had thought that I would be one voice
in a sea of stories in an hour of testimonies, but now
I felt more like the keynote speaker. She told me that
nobody would be mad if I changed my mind. She
said that I didn't have to share. But I've noticed that
if I don't follow divine instructions then they will just
spiral back around again (and probably on a bigger
scale) so I figured I'd just get it over with. The only way
to be done with this was to just do it. Sometimes you
just have to go through it.

After all that work of learning to tune in to my
intuition and follow my gut, I learned that sometimes
our gut is stuck in old trauma patterns and our own
intuition is not always acting in our own best interest.
My gut and my ancestors were screaming that it wasn't
safe and my inner voice was telling me about all the
horrible things that could happen, but I chose to listen

to the instructions that were coming from a source that I knew could see further. I knew that I needed to be pushed a little bit to take the steps that were moving me down a path that I couldn't even see yet. But this time when I felt pushed, I kind of felt like that meant that God had my back. I was shaking like a leaf but I just kept reading. I was looking at the little kids in the crowd and I knew that I had written the fairy tale version for a reason so that some listeners would be able to hear it on the surface and others could understand the deeper meaning. When it was over, they led a march through the city and then we all went inside for a candlelight vigil. A young woman actually gathered up the courage to step away from the safety of her group of college friends, and stepped out into the circle, and crossed the room to thank me for speaking. That was all she said, but her eyes and her actions said so much more. I saw my younger self in her. I'm not sure what else will come from the ripples that went out from that night and I need to stop holding on so tightly and open my hand and just let it go, but one girl's courageous journey across the room was enough for me to know that it was worth it.

Maybe my story will inspire you to take one more step on your journey. Maybe it will help you learn to tune in to your own inner guidance. Maybe you will open up and learn to say "yes." Maybe you will find the courage to say "no." Maybe you will learn that you can break a pattern without being shattered into a million pieces. Maybe your old self will be broken open and you will find something beautiful that was waiting to be revealed. Maybe you will just know that no matter where the journey takes you, in each of those moments, you are never alone.

Blessings on *Your* Journey.

Magdalena

Appendix:

Energy Centers	Ages
1. Root (hips, base of spine) Color: Red	0, 7, 14, 21, 28, 35, 42
2. Sacrum (lower abdomen, sexual and reproductive organs) Color: Orange	1, 8, 15, 22, 29, 36, 43
3. Solar Plexus (upper abdomen, gut, stomach) Color: Yellow	2, 9, 16, 23, 30, 37, 44
4. Heart/Lungs/ Breasts (*Balance point between lower and upper chakras*) Color: Green	3, 10, 17, 24, 31, 38, 45
5. Neck/Throat/Arms Color: Blue	4, 11, 18, 25, 32, 39, 46
6.Third Eye, Brain, Pituitary and Pineal Glands Color: Indigo	5, 12, 19, 26, 33, 40, 47
7. Crown, Muscles, Nerves, Skeleton, Skin Color: Violet	6, 13, 20, 27, 34, 41, 48

Mothering Mission	Developmental Focus
Physically: Healthy and Alive	Home, Comfort, Grounded, Supported, and Safe
Financially: Secure and Responsible	Survival, Self-Worth, Control, and ability to create in the physical world
Socially: Aware and Respectful	Personal Power, self-esteem, identity, and confidence
Passionately: Loving and Purposeful	Balance, Connection, True to yourself, Soul Purpose, Care-taking
Emotionally: Safe and Heard	Expression (creating art, writing, dancing, Speaking your Truth)
Mentally: Stimulated and Challenged	Intuition (inner knowing), reconnect with true self, passion, vision, clarity
Spiritually: Connected and Seeking	Inspiration, spirituality, receiving guidance, connection to the divine

References:

1. Backstein, Karen. *The Blind Men and the Elephant.* Hello Reader! Level 3 (Paperback). Cartwheel; 1992. ISBN-10: 0590458132

2. Wilbanks, Brett. The Muscle of the Soul May be Triggering your Fear and Anxiety. Waking Times; 2015. http://www.wakingtimes.com/2015/06/02/the-muscle-of-the-soul-may-be-triggering-your-fear-and-anxiety/

3. Supported Birth. The Real Story of Twilight Sleep and How it Shaped Obstetrics and Hospital Birth. Available at: http://www.supportedbirth.com/articles/twilight-sleep-childbirth-history

4. Centers for Disease Control website. About Behavioral Risk Factor Surveillance System ACE Data. Available at: https://www.cdc.gov/violenceprevention/acestudy/ace_brfss.html

5. Colino, Stacy. The Health Benefits of Hugging. 2016. Available at: https://health.usnews.com/health-news/health-wellness/articles/2016-02-03/the-health-benefits-of-hugging

6. Murgia, Madhumita. How Stress Affects your Brain. [Video for Ted-Ed]. Available at: https://www.youtube.com/watch?v=WuyPuH9ojCE see full lesson: https://ed.ted.com/lessons/how-stress-affects-your-brain-madhumita-murgia

7. The University of Minnesota Monarch Lab. Monarch Biology and Natural History. ©2016. Available at: https://monarchlab.org/biology-and-research/biology-and-natural-history/

8. The Parable of the Good Sower. The Gospel of Matthew 13:1-23. The Holy Bible, New International Version (NIV.) International Bible Society. 1984.

9. Schutte, Daniel L. "Behold the Wood" New Dawn Music. ©1976. Available at: https://www.danschuttemusic.com

10. Zemach, Margot. *The Little Red Hen.* Originally published 1942. Little Golden Book Series. Random House Children's Books, 2001. ISBN 13: 9780307960306

11. Kent, Jack. *The Caterpillar and the Pollywog.* Reprint edition. Aladdin; 1985. ISBN-10: 9780671662813

12. Stevenson, Mary. "Footprints in the Sand" poem. Originally written 1936. Copyright 1984. Available at: http://www.footprints-inthe-sand.com

13. LeLoup, Jean-Yves. *The Gospel of Mary Magdalene.* Inner Traditions/Bear & Company, 2002. ISBN-13: 9780892819119

14. Myss, Caroline. *Energy Anatomy: The Science of Personal Power, Spirituality and Health.* [Audio CD] Sounds True; 2001. ISBN-10: 1564558800 Available at: https://www.soundstrue.com/store/energy-anatomy-3805.html

15. Tan, Amy. Author. More information available at: https://www.amytan.net/

16. Godspell. *By My Side.* Lyrics by Jay Hamburger. Music by Peggy Gordon. Pressed by Bestway Products Inc.; 1971. Available at: http://www.musicalschwartz.com/godspell-peggy-gordon.htm

17. Thomashauer, Regena. "Mama Gena's School of Womanly Arts." Information available at: http://www.mamagenas.com/about-us/

18. Shinoda-Bolen, Jean, M.D. *Crossing to Avalon: A Woman's Midlife Quest for the Sacred Feminine.* Harper Collins Publishers, 2004. ISBN-10: 0062502727

19. Zimmer Bradley, Marion. *The* Mists of Avalon. Knopf Book Club, 1982. ISBN-10: 113562674X. [Audiobook] ASIN: B008CM40B8. [DVD]: Directed by Uli Edel. Warner Home Video, 2012. ASIN: B007TBJUW2

20. Williamson, Marianne. "Our Deepest Fear." Available at: https://marianne.com/ [Godspell version] "Tower of Babel" Prologue. 2001. Available at: http://musicandthearts.com/prologue_(tower_of_bable_2001).html

21. Educational Insights. "Royal Rescue" game. ASIN: B0012XRVVU Available at: www.amazon.com/Educational-Insights-2956-Royal-Rescue/dp/B0012XRVVU

22. Auel, Jean M. Earth's Children series. Available at: http://www.jeanauel.com/books.php

23. Chapman, Michael. *Clan of the Cave Bear* [DVD]. Warner Home Video, 1999. ASIN: 0790742764

24. Antevasin, Mb. The Meaning of Antevasin. mbantevasin.

com/2014/04/04/the-meaning-of-antevasin/

25. "Daughters of Earth" gathering founded in 2005. And "The Red Tent Temple Movement" founded in 2006. By Alisa Starkweather. Information available at: http://redtenttemplemovement.com/

26. *The Red Tent* by Anita Diamant Paperback September 15, 1998. St. Martin's Press. ASIN: B004TMT7OK Information at: http://anitadiamant.com/books/the-red-tent/overview/

27. *The Borning Room* by Paul Fleischman. HarperCollins, 1991. ISBN: 978-0-06-023762-2

28. Map of Red Tents. Available at: http://www.redtent-movie.com/red_tents_near_you.html

29. *"The Things We Don't Talk About: Women's Stories from the Red Tent"* Documentary Film by Isadora Gabrielle Leidenfrost PhD. Available at: *http://www.redtentmovie.com/*

30. *Women's Bodies, Women's Wisdom: Creating Physical and Emotional Health and Healing.* Christiane Northrup, MD 1994. Bantam Books. ISBN: 0-553-37466-4.

31. The Zentangle® Method created by Rick Roberts and Maria Thomas. More information available at: https://www.zentangle.com/

32. *The Law of Attraction: The Basics of the Teachings of Abraham* by Esther and Jerry Hicks. Hay House September 25, 2006. ISBN-10: 1401912273

33. Articles available at: https://www.entrepreneur.com/

34. Brad Yates EFT videos https://www.youtube.com/user/eftwizard Information available at: http://www.tapwith-brad.com

35. *The Wizard's Wish: Or, How He Made the Yuckies Go Away - A Story About the Magic in You* Paperback –Createspace July 24, 2010 by Brad Yates ISBN-10:1451570902 Available at: https://www.amazon.com/Wizards-Wish-Yuckies-Story-About/dp/1451570902

36. "What is EFT tapping?" The Tapping Solution. 2007. Available at: https://www.thetappingsolution.com/what-is-eft-tapping/

37. *Going on a Bear Hunt* by Michael Rosen. Aladdin Paperbacks reprint edition. 2003. ISBN-10: 0689853491

38. *Entering the Castle: Finding the Inner Path to God and Your Soul's Purpose* by Caroline Myss 2008. 2008. ISBN-10: 074325533X

39. *The Interior Castle by St. Teresa of Avila* (Author), E. Allison Peers (Translator) originally published 1946. (Dover Thrift Editions) Paperback – December 17, 2007. ISBN-10:0486461459

40. The Gifts of the Holy Spirit: St. Paul's Letter to the Corinthians (1Cor 12.) The Holy Bible, New International Version (NIV.) International Bible Society. 1984.

41. Consider the lilies. The Gospel of Matthew (6:25-34) Luke (12:22.) The Holy Bible, New International Version (NIV.) International Bible Society. 1984.

42. The "Seven Generations Principle" from the Haudeno-saunee people. Available at: http://www.pbs.org/war-rior/content/timeline/opendoor/roleOfChief.html

43. *Enemy of the People* by Henrik Ibsen. 1882. Dover Thrift Editions. 1999. ISBN-10: 0486406571

44. "The U.S. in World War II: See the Posters that Urged Secrecy" By Albinko Hasic Dec. 8, 2016 Available at: http://time.com/4591841/loose-lips-sink-ships-posters/

45. "Here I am, Lord" Dan Schutte 1981 Available at: http://www.danschutte.com

46. Take Back the Night® charitable 501©3 Foundation. Information available at: https://takebackthenight.org

About the Author

M.B. (Michelle) Antevasin is a mother, a teacher, and a healer and she works at the intersection of science and spirituality to break patterns and promote healing. Michelle has been studying the science of Health and Wellness for over twenty years. She has a Bachelor's degree in Biology and a Masters of Public Health in Epidemiology and is a Certified Science Teacher.

While raising her 4 children she became an accredited La Leche League Leader and a Professionally Trained Birth Doula and recently completed a 3-year Energy Healing training and is a Certified Family Trauma Professional. She currently runs her own health consultation business and is a Professor of Business, Health and Science. She volunteers with Children and Families in her community and she works to end patterns of abuse and trauma by sharing her own healing journey through her writing and she brings to her classes and workshops her experience as a teacher, a mother, a survivor and a healer. Michelle also holds support groups monthly and is available for private healing sessions.